DATE YOUR CLIENTS

written by

MARK YOUNG

© Copyright 2022 by Mark Young. All rights reserved.

It is not legal to reproduce, duplicate, or transmit any part of this document in either electronic means or printed format.

Recording of this publication is strictly prohibited.

This book is dedicated to all the hope-filled

entrepreneurs who are fighting daily to

make their American dreams a reality.

The harder you work, the luckier you'll get.

I promise.

Contents

FOREWORD 1
    AUTHOR'S DISCLAIMER AND INVITATION 4
PART I: They Meet 9
    CHAPTER 1: MAKE 'EM SWIPE RIGHT 11
    CHAPTER 2: FINDING YOUR "TYPE" 23
    CHAPTER 3: THE FIRST DATE 35
    CHAPTER 4: THE FIRST DATE (PART DEUX) 51
    CHAPTER 5: WHEN MINUTE 16 MATTERS MOST 73
PART II: The Chase 97
    CHAPTER 6: CHIVALRY IS NOT DEAD 99
    CHAPTER 7: PHEROMONE-INFUSED PERFUMES ARE EN VOGUE 109
    CHAPTER 8: LEFT ON READ 123
    CHAPTER 9: IT'S ALL ABOUT TRUST 137
    CHAPTER 10: MEETING THE FAMILY 149
    CHAPTER 11: MOVING IN TOGETHER 163
    CHAPTER 12: FRIDAY NIGHT IS DATE NIGHT 179
PART III: The Moment of Truth 191
    CHAPTER 13: THE FIRST FIGHT 193
    CHAPTER 14: THE WALK OF SHAME 207
    CHAPTER 15: THE BREAKUP 219
    CHAPTER 16: NETFLIX AND CHILL 233
    CHAPTER 17: COMMITMENT ISSUES 247
    CHAPTER 18: SETTLING DOWN 259
CONCLUSION: 273
ARE YOU READY FOR A HAPPY ENDING? 273
BIBLIOGRAPHY 275
ABOUT THE AUTHOR 277

FOREWORD

by Rusty Humphries
Nationally Syndicated Radio Talk Show Host

I've had a robust career, to say the very least. As a top-rated radio personality, best-selling author, music producer, actor, and talent coach, I have been blessed to have worked with some major entertainers throughout my life. People like Will Smith, Mark Wahlberg, Ryan Seacrest, Dick Clark, Casey Kasem, Rush Limbaugh, George Michael, Adam Sandler, Chris Farley, Suzanne Somers, Chuck Woolery, Amy Grant, Tony Orlando, Michael Damian, Gov. Sarah Palin, Wilson-Phillips, Orson Scott Card, former VP Mike Pence, and hundreds more, as well as major corporations like Coca-Cola, Mercedes-Benz, Ford Motor Company (and to quote the band *Journey*, "it goes on and on, and on, and on").

I've had backstage access to the greatest thinkers, promoters, entertainers, and storytellers of our time, and as you can imagine, I can be a little jaded at times. I can't tell you the number of times I've heard, "I'm going to write a book!" I try to be encouraging, but most people just talk, and very few do.

But on occasion, the book gets written, and then I'm asked to read it. Now, if someone asks me to read their book, I'm a bit hesitant, because I usually have better things to do, but most importantly most books are ... shall we say ... "just not very good." It can be a chore to suffer through bad writing - especially if it's a friend, who says they just want your "honest opinion." (Also, note, they don't want your honest opinion. They only want your praise.)

So, my friend Mark Young sends me a book and asks me to read it. I open it up and see the title: *Date Your Clients*. My first thought was a flashback to Harvey Korman in the Mel Brooks film *Blazing Saddles*. "Kinky!"

(By the way, if you're a bit "woke" and haven't seen Blazing Saddles, you might want to skip that one).

After a quick chuckle, I thought, "Wait! This is Mark Young. This guy is super smart, and probably not looking to be a serial sexual harasser with major HR problems. Maybe - just maybe - he's going someplace with this." So, I gave it a read.

Now, in my radio days, I read many books. I mean, *a lot* of books. Unsolicited, I've probably been given an average of five books a *day* to read (not to imply that I read them all). (That's 25 books a week x 4 weeks a month x 12 months in a year, totaling 1,200 books per year. Multiply that by 25 years on radio and we're talking about 30,000 books!)

That's a lot of books!

Thinking I was the world's largest consumer of books, I did a little research to test this theory. As fate would have it, I was wrong, but I learned who *is* the largest buyer of books in the world. Any guesses? Amazon? Barnes and Noble? Costco?

Nope! It's the toilet paper companies, so they can shred the books and let you wipe in comfort.

The correlation? Most of the books I am asked to read probably deserve to be Charmin. Of those 30,000 books, very few have stuck in my mind, and an even smaller number have taught me something I've remembered throughout my life.

***Date Your Clients* is that kind of book. (*Not the toilet paper kind; the good kind*.)**

As I began to read this book, I was not only pleasantly surprised, but I started *learning* some important things. For instance:

- Why it is important to think of your client relationships as a courtship (but in a wholly platonic way!).
- Why it is important NOT to take every client, even if you need the money.
- How to work through disagreements with clients and make the working relationship better than ever.

It's not only a fun, interesting read, but an important book for anyone who deals with other humans and wants to improve their effectiveness.

My applause to Mark for this book. Guaranteed, when you're done, you'll applaud too, and will see the type of value that relational intelligence can bring to any business relationship. It is not a surprise why Mark sets the standard for client service in his field. And it's no surprise because his clients all agree.

Author's Disclaimer and Invitation

If, by the title alone, you're thinking that this book sounds unconventional; you're right. It isn't for the faint of heart, if we're being honest, because its sole purpose is revisiting many of the most embarrassing, traumatic, and wish-you-could-forget moments from your dumpster fire of a love life – then applying all those painful lessons directly to your professional life. Even if your life took the "marry my high school sweetheart" track, it's not always been wine and roses, I'd bet, so pony up and let's ride.

You see, my contention is that relationships, regardless of their context, follow predictable patterns. And, as you'll hopefully learn throughout this inked masterpiece, there is no point in learning a lesson twice. If you've learned it in one area of life, that knowledge (and by knowledge, I mean "shame, embarrassment, guilt, joy, heartbreak, and butterflies") can be applied to virtually any other situation.

Truth is, we are always learning – like it or not. And, as much as I hate to admit it, we likely learn the most when things go wrong. The more wrong, the more learning, I suppose. Through dips and turns, twists of fate, and the retelling of some of my own guilt-soaked illustrations, we're going to cling to failure and use it as the very manure which will grow you into the success that you've always dreamed of being.

Whether you're a business owner, business manager, or even an aspiring troubadour, there's something to be learned between the covers of this wit-filled text. So, grab a beer. You may need it. This raw (sometimes very raw) journey is going to need some honesty. I'll start the conversation, but it is ultimately yours to finish. Introspect and reminisce - and judge if you must – but, at this point, we're just a couple of friends having a beer and discussing life.

I love entrepreneurs. Like, you have no idea how much I love them. It's almost an unhealthy obsession. They're crazy. I mean, nothing about becoming a business owner makes sense. It's the exact opposite of a low-stress, high-security life. In fact, it's like working a 90-hour week, just to put all the money on 14-RED, and the odds are in the house's favor. But we play anyway.

(And I'll include those folks who I'll lovingly call "intra-preneurs" as well. They are the folks who hop on board of someone else's "0-to-1" and take it from a 1 to a 10. You know who you are. You make it rain and make the "big guy" look good. You are the real heroes, by the way. All the guts and – usually – none of the glory.)

Raw truth here: I am so tired of everyone with a social media account trying to become a consultant on successful business practices. Like, you're 12 ½ years old, Junior. And your experience isn't even as deep as my interest in your high score on Fortnight. For the sake of Pete, can we please stop talking about #levelingup and #thehustlelife?

I get what Junior and his friends are doing, but let me ask you honestly: As a business owner or manager, do you really believe that the key to your explosive success is going to be found in one more morning inspiration? As a business professional, are you really lacking that kind of guidance? Is that what fixes the P/L?

I contend that too many business owners are looking from someone to teach them how to "do business," when, in fact, they already have the experience they need; it just looks a little different than they expect. You aren't giving yourself enough credit here, and I'm going to show you why.

(At this point, picture Glinda the Good Witch gently speaking to you: "You've always had the power, my dear. You just had to learn it for yourself.")

My business? Advertising. I am the CEO and chief strategist of an advertising agency called *Ryze* (www.ryzeagency.com). I spend my days meeting with entrepreneurs, mostly, and listening to their stories. Sometimes of success. Sometimes of failure. Sometimes of them trying to convince me that they already know what's going on. The stories aren't so different though. They're all about struggle and grit and inspiration and determination. They're human stories wrapped up in innovative packaging – and my job is to gently unwrap these fragile tales and get them consumer-ready.

Many of the stories I share here may seem extreme, but they're all true. And while I may make light of the craziest of *faux pas*, I assure you that each relational error contained herein was all made with the best of intentions – typically. Business, after all, can feel like tap dancing in a mine field, but the point of our time here is to learn the ways in which we can benefit from our own – or other people's – mistakes and kick-ball-change our way on to greener pastures.

Dating in the Workplace

Taboo, right?

Or is it?

As you'll learn through this, "tutorial," we'll call it, the same skills you've learned in the complicated, yet culturally-relevant, world of Tinder are directly applicable to the business world. The same lessons you've been learning the hard way since you were a hormone-saturated, pimpled adolescent are the same lessons that will drive you to entrepreneurial success.

As you will soon see, each chapter of this heavenly-inspired prose is written like a slow-motion stroll through some of the worst moments of your life (or, as fate would have it, mine). And, trust me, if you haven't lived these exact experiences, you know someone who has. We're going to dodge, dip, duck, dive, and dodge through fifty-one shades of awkward (notice my attention to detail and not wanting to 'err on the wrong side of copyrights). Then, after the dust settles, we're going to see that it was all just a bootcamp for the inevitable success that we'll call "you." (Imagine me swooning at the feigned sentiment I just added to your life.)

Step by step through the ever-meandering river of relationship management, we're going to draw some parallels to your professional success and connect the dots between relational maturity and business success. Don't believe me? Follow along.

Let's take a stroll down memory lane to some of the worst moments of your youth, reminiscing on all of the times you struck out – then we'll relish in the would-be failures and raise our victory flags high, as we finally realize the relational equity you were earning all along without even knowing it.

So, buckle up, because you're about to ride shotgun on this self-diagnosed ADHD Matterhorn of my mind. Stay alert.

PART I: They Meet

On your public image.

Chapter 1: Make 'Em Swipe Right
(Tinder Reference #2)

We'll start right here at the beginning.

There you are, sitting at home on a Friday night, building your online dating profile (praying to all things holy that nobody in your social circle ever gets "matched" with you). Forgive yourself. We've all been there.

And now the big question: Which picture on your phone makes you look absolutely *nothing* like you look in real life? You don't want it to look like a selfie (because that's the self-promotion). You don't want it to look too staged (because people will just think you're posing). Damn it!

Finally, you find just the right photo. Edit it. Edit it again. Add a filter. And ... post.

Oh, gosh. Now they want a bio. You get to choose the five words that describe you best, Boo. And, predictably, here they are: "Loyal. Fun. Honest. Family. God."

Congratulations, you just used the exact same description as 80.4% of all online dating profiles. Way to stand out from the crowd. I hope you chose that photo wisely, because a lot is hinging on it to set you apart now.

Digital dating. Your personal brand on display for the world to see – and any eligible bachelor or bachelorette will decide on whether to engage you exclusively from that profile. That pic. Those five words. The number of hours – even minutes or seconds – it takes you to respond to a message. It's all part of that brand you're projecting to the world. And, if you're interested in hearing the worst news ever, I'll break it to you gently here.

Wait for it.

You will never know why someone didn't swipe right. Ever. Repeat: ever. Your potential soul mate kept scrolling and you will never know it. Talk about a butterfly effect. That one poorly-selected photo just cost you a dog, a minivan, and a white picket fence. And here you are, one filter away from happiness – and you don't even know it, because you're still waiting for your first mobile connection, oblivious that it slipped through your fingers.

Oblivious. Hmm, I like that word. Unaware. Unmindful. Unsuspecting. It's loaded with meaning.

And do you know what it reminds me of? Small business owners who could, potentially, have the best product or service in the world, but lack the ability to build an even remotely-appealing persona online. They settle for a website built by a nephew from his parents' basement (because it was cheaper). They settle for Vistaprint marketing materials (designed on the site's graphics tool, of course). They settle for clip art in a Photoshop world and are *oblivious* to the entire left-swiping world around them.

Pass. Pass. Pass.

Top secret newsflash, friends: Entrepreneurs typically become entrepreneurs because they are *really* good at something *very* specific. And, typically, it isn't sales. They're the chefs who start restaurants, but never learned how to get patrons through the doors. It may be the best meal ever prepared, but if never leaves the kitchen, what does it matter? If everyone is swiping left, they'll never know that you're the greatest human on the third rock from the sun. Meanwhile, you're oblivious.

I hope you're following the parallel here. If not, I'm afraid you may be more oblivious than I once feared. We may need to talk. But, for the rest of you, let's continue.

Every day, I spend time on the phone with potential clients and/or would-be business partners and they explain to me that they have "the best product on the market." It is immediately, with 94% certainty, followed by the phrase: "... if people only knew about it, they'd ..." (You can fill in the blank.)

Yes, Barbara, that's true. And if everyone got to meet you in person and taste your world-famous brownies, you could stop spending your Friday night building an online dating profile. So, what are you going to do about it? I'll tell you. We're going to spend as many nights as necessary to polish our brand (whether personal or professional), to add the curb appeal required to get you noticed.

You're not failing at making a good product, I'm sure. Or offering a great service. You're failing at getting enough people to know about it. Your one goal in building that profile is to get noticed. It's a hook. Just as you're not expecting your dating profile to serve as a marriage proposal, your business' public presence doesn't need to close a sale. It simply needs to provide enough intrigue for a potential consumer to want to learn more.

For a business, it's a website. It's signage. It's a television commercial. It's your sales rep. Ask yourself, when is the first time that a potential customer would encounter your business? That's the moment that your consumer makes the decision to explore a potential relationship with you.

If you look cheap, you are cheap. If you look disorganized, you are disorganized. If you look really new, you are really new. Perception is reality in this game of first impressions. So, my friends, pony up on the curb appeal, because some of your stock values are plummeting, and you're sitting around waiting for a phone to ring ... *oblivious*.

"But," you ask, "what if I just don't know what to do?"

Great question. And an even greater answer is on its way, with a little bit of audience participation required, simply to test your intuition.

Question: What do I do if I don't know how to market myself / my business? (Select one answer from the list below.)

A. Talk to your nephew who is "really good at computers" and see if he can build you a website.

B. Bury your head in the sand, because things you don't understand are really scary and should be ignored.

C. Take to social media and post as many inspirational "live, laugh, love" posts as you can find on Pinterest, knowing that your 34 followers will all be inspired and tell their friends about you.

D. Hire a damn professional who knows how to actually *sell* something.

If you didn't select "D" as your answer, we really have problems here. Well, you do. I'm good. But I'm here to help, so I'm making *your* problems *my* problems. *Mi casa es su casa.*

Look back to option "D," because there is *one* word in *italics*, and it is imperative that we talk about how this answer could still lead you astray. The nuance in answer "D" is that the professional you hire must know how to *sell* something. Mere "art" and the "art of selling" are two totally different disciplines. Two skill sets entirely. And, as crazy as this sounds, one seldom overlaps the other. Pretty pictures never made me open my wallet.

Sidebar Story

I had a sidebar conversation with a guy last night while guest speaking at a conference. He was asking me, offline, if I would look at his website with him. I had done an initial consultation with him a month or so ago, in which I was fairly brutal ("truthful") about the state of his online presence. (It was *really* bad.) No matter what I said to him on the telephone, however, he would reply and tell me that he already knew whatever I suggested and the updated version of the website was due out in two weeks including those fixes. (My first reaction was to suggest ending the call, as I *clearly* had nothing to tell him that he didn't already know. But I'm nicer than that. Usually. Well, not often, but I must have been in a good mood.)

Last night, I was introduced to the *new and improved* site. It sucked as much as the first one.

So, here we are, standing outside of this conference center with a laptop and he's expecting me to critique his new website on the spot like a trick pony.

"What do you think of the new site?" he asked. "Do you have any thoughts?"

Do I have thoughts? Is the pope catholic? I have thoughts.

The conversation went something like this:

ME (kindly): "Well, I can say that the new site is much 'prettier' than the old site. You have aesthetically made a lot of improvements."

Him: "But, do you think it fixes the problems you pointed out the last time?"

ME (still holding on to my real opinion): "It certainly is a lot prettier."

Him: "But, do you think it fixes the problems you pointed out the last time?"

ME: "Honestly? No. It is the exact same package with a different bow. You have focused all your attention on the art and none of your attention on the science. That's why you spent the last half hour complaining to that lady over there about how you can't get anyone to buy your product. You're spending your entire marketing budget trying to drive traffic to a broken website, rather than spending the money to fix the website in the first place. Now you don't have any money left – *and* you still have a broken website."

Color me offended, but it never ceases to amaze me that everyone thinks that they are marketing geniuses. Everyone who knows how to program a website *must* be an expert on the psychology of sales. Makes total sense, right? Similarly, I'll ask my auto mechanic to perform my upcoming heart surgery. And I'll see if my attorney has any free time to swing by and replace my hot water tank.

Back to that big "D" we were discussing above.

You need a *professional*. But not a professional at website programming. You need a professional who knows how to make *sales*.

Have you ever seen the movie *Hitch*, with Will Smith? He was a dating coach. He knew how to *sell* something – even something undesirable. He wasn't a fashion designer, nor a barber. He just knew how to put the package together. You need Hitch. Call me "Hitch."

Personal Confession

I remember sitting at a restaurant with a friend one time when the topic of online dating came up. It's always an awkward topic, online dating, because, although it has become so mainstream, folks are still self-conscious about seeming too desperate or unable to meet a potential mate in a "more traditional" way. Bag it. I spend more time texting my family than having dinner with them, and more time sending emails than making phone calls, so knock off your Mennonite-like oppression and *cyber up* already.

Continuing, my friend suggested a new dating app where he was "having some huge wins." Classy, I know. So, I joined. Naturally. And, while this next passage is not an actual transcription, the paraphrase is uncanny.

SJ: "Okay, so you get to put in six pictures of yourself. But be careful which six you choose."

ME: "What about this one? Or this one?"

SJ: "No. There's a formula. You have six opportunities to show all sides of yourself. And she'll draw conclusions from these six images. You need one good profile photo which makes you look your best. Serious is best. Then, pick one photo that shows you smiling big, like laughing, and put that one next so you have range of emotions there. Then, do one with you doing something silly or funny. Use two group photos, which makes you seem like you have friends – I mean, you do have friends, but let her know that. And then use a picture of you with a kid, but be sure that you put on the profile that it isn't your kid. Girls love pics with kids."

ME: "..."

Frankly, just writing the story makes me laugh about it all over again. He knew the profile "formula." He knew exactly how to choose the right combination of photos to get me the optimal number of impressions and *right swipes*. I'll spare you the qualifying questions and text he suggested for an optimal profile, but you can imagine that it was extensive and well-curated.

SJ knew exactly how to create an online brand. Perfectly – even if he wasn't selling a great product or offering a great service.

From the CEO's Desk

It wasn't too long ago that I had a client come to me frustrated because they were running television commercials but were not having much success getting traffic to their website. The product was a family of health and beauty accessories. "We're just not noticing a bump in traffic to justify the advertising spend," said the director of marketing. "Maybe people just don't watch TV anymore."

Fail.

You'll notice that it was easier for the client to believe that "people don't watch TV anymore" than it was to believe that they had done a poor job of representing their brand. It was an immediate jump to a conclusion which held the marketing director blameless.

Again, fail.

We spent a lot of time together that day and I was able to help that client correct a fundamental problem with their messaging. We walked through the basics of solution-based marketing and all that jazz, and I think I got through.

The client had provided a pretty picture. They had one serious photo. One smiling ... just kidding.

But really, they had an attractive commercial which gave some really valuable information. The message had no hook though. There was no reason to learn more or explore further. It was vanilla.

When a consumer visited their website, it was equally as bland. There was no call to action. No reason to act today. No clear indication as to which of their dozens of products a person should choose. It was my contention that the customer just found their message to be ... "nice." (And in the marketing world, that's about the same as being the girl with the "great sense of humor.")

Sadly, the director of marketing was much more willing to blame *the television*, rather than own the problem. Craziness, right? Much like the people who complain that "there are just no good men/women left."

Perchance, there are, but you're just not doing the right things to attract them? [gasps]

Did I just say that?

Ryze-ing to the Occasion

At our agency, we deal with this all the time. All day, every day, we are approached by people with products and services which are in search of a marketing agency to help them "get to the next level" or "take things global." (The clichés kill me. Seriously. Slow death.)

I get to spend my professional life telling people that their babies are ugly. And, what is the worst part of this job, you may or may not ask? Sometimes the worst stories of online marketing failures are OURS.

There. I admitted it. We are like the starving baker. Like the cobbler's kids.

We do some of our worst work on the brands that we have invested in (yes, we own some of our own brands). And the reason is simple, really: We are so close to the situation that we lose all perspective. Like those clients who know *so much* about their products that they just speak in industry colloquialisms, we do the same thing when we are not careful. We just "know," so we quit explaining. We quit selling.

Internally, one of our best practices is to always have what I call "story time."

As an example, when a web designer and/or developer proposes a new site design, I (or someone else on our team) starts the conversation with a little bit of roleplaying.

"Before you show me the new site, tell me what I already know about you. I'm the consumer. How did I hear about you? Did I see you on TV and this is where I'm landing? Did I look for you? Did you look for me? Have I visited your site before? Have I asked for information?"

This line of questioning forces objectivity. It focuses the conversation on the intended audience, rather than the designer. Know your audience.

And, if you want to talk about the dating equivalent of this advice, go look at your online profile (or find a mirror, for heaven's sake), and ask yourself, *objectively*: "Would you date you?"

Today's Lessons Learned

- Know the difference between *being* online and *selling* online.
- It is painful to think that your online brand is *not* doing what you want it to do. *It is even more* painful to realize that your online brand is doing things you don't want it to do.
- It is imperative for you to seek objective advice from people who are not emotionally connected to you or your brand. People who love you are seldom honest. They are jaded and want to spare your feelings. And, frankly, why would they want to be the person who offends you? Hire a jackass who speaks truth.
- All companies (and individuals) need to stop and take an objective look at their online presence. If you're not proud, rebuild.

Now, Ask Yourself

- Self, what is the personal brand that you want to portray – I mean *really portray* – to the world?
- Self, does the brand you portray - online or otherwise - represent who you *want* to be? Socially? Personally? Professionally?
- Self, when faced with rejection, do you tend to blame others, or do you take the time to reflect on how you could have contributed?
- Self, do you have people in your life who will help take off the blinders and be honest with you? Who are they?
- Self, did you just read these questions out loud and place a very dramatic pause after the word "self" in each question? I may be judging you (and laughing a little).

On creating demand.

Chapter 2: Finding Your "Type"

Now that you're getting noticed, the world feels like a virtual carnival of options. Whatever your pleasure, it seems as if the opportunities are endless. It's like your chances of success are better than a pie surviving less than 32 minutes in Rosie O'Donnell's kitchen. The only thing in scarcity, it seems, is your time.

So, Punkin, let's talk about some focus here. And I mean some good, old fashioned, take-the-whole-bottle-of-Ritalin kind of focus.

Back to our online dating metaphors, shall we? I like those. And, like it or not, you relate to them better than you'd care to publicly admit.

We've talked a bit about the epic swipe right, but what about the dreaded swipe left? We've learned it well, I'm afraid. Right = Good. Left = Bad. If there's anything you learned from the last chapter, it is that you want them to always swipe right. Here is the secret to right-swiping goodness ... [insert pregnant pause] ... you're going to love this ... [insert annoying delay of game] ... are you ready? [insert dramatic start of a new paragraph]

You want them to swipe right because now YOU get to do the pickin'.

The best part about having options is that you're now the one with the power.

Remember the first time you went on a date with an ugly guy or girl (whatever your liking)? You were almost cockily (is that even a word?) confident. For reals. Why? Because you were the hunter, instead of the hunted. You knew darned well that if you didn't even return a text for >24 hours, you'd *still* get a second date. Why? Because you were the catch.

The other guy/gal swiped right.

You hesitated before you swiped. Then you finally swiped right and figured you'd let the Tinder gods decide. And, while two wrongs will never make a right, two rights always make a match. No fate involved. It felt casual, really.

Whether you've ever been involved in this online dating scene or not, you know the story. Sing along with me ... "*Tale as old as time ...*" You know it.

My advice: *Never be the beast.*

Always be the one with options. The man who isn't afraid of saying "no" is the most powerful guy in the room, after all. And if the thought of being that guy doesn't start a party in your pants, check your pulse.

But, as they say, with much power comes much responsibility. (Thank you, Aunt Mae. We miss you.)

So, here you are, potential clients everywhere. They're swiping right like it's their job. But here you are, still bound by space and time, only having 24 hours in your marvelously busy days. Cloning still being a less-than-reliable option, the only choice is to invest those hours in the relationship / partner / match which is most likely to yield the highest ROI, right? (So romantic, I know.)

Gone are your days of desperately closing the deal with the only person who called. You've tipped the scales in your favor and get to start making the decisions. And, as a bit of a personal inventory, I invite you to take a deeper dive into your own professional memoires.

Answering honestly, make some notes. Irrespective of your current business endeavors, ask yourself these questions:

1. Who is the client I did the best work for? (If you're a wedding planner, what was the best wedding you ever planned?)

2. Why is that? (Is it because they matched your personal interest? Or the bride let you do things the way you preferred, rather than giving you detailed marching orders.)

3. If there were one thing you'd prefer to never do again, professionally speaking, of course, what would it be? (Now imagine a world where that thing doesn't even exist.)

4. And if you were asked to give a speech about some aspect of your current career, what would the topic be? (Everyone can be in their underwear for this segment of today's programming, but careful to keep that visual contained.) There is something about what you do that makes you keep coming back for more.

5. What is it about what you do that doesn't feel like work? (Call it "Netflix and chill," but some dates just flow better than others.)

As a serial entrepreneur, nobody understands your struggle more than I do. Small businesses are all about loving the one you're with. We become experts on the client who is willing to sign. We reinvent and cannibalize ourselves as often as necessary to keep the rent paid. Why wouldn't you? Sometimes it all just works out, right?

Yeah, that's true. Sometimes it works out. Other times, you spend years of your finite existence trying to force something that *ain't ever gonna work*. And why? Because it's better than having nobody.

True, I guess. A business without a single client doesn't thrive very often. But why does the default opposite of "*wrong client*" have to be "*no client*"? How about painting that picture a little differently. Can't the opposite of "wrong client" be "*right client*"?

Divorce courts are overrun by couples who figured that they could "figure out their differences" after they were married. And I'm not so naïve to believe that navigating a marriage is easy work, but I expect you to not be naïve enough to believe that managing a business with an *elephant-in-the-room client* is any easier.

They're demanding.

They're volatile.

They're unpredictable.

They're all of the things that keep you up at night worrying that you're one emotional decision away from ruin.

If any of that sounds familiar you're in good company.

Back to the point of our chapter though: Knowing Your Type. The screening process is a wonderful thing.

1. Be good enough that you have options.
2. Rank your options by likelihood to fit your *preferences*. (Hear me here. *Preferences*. Not based on financial gain, ego, or "make sense" decisions. *Preferences*. Rank your options based on personal preference.)
3. Now, spend 80% of your time working on the clients who made the top 20% of your list.

I'm telling you to get that little black book out (or its digital equivalent for my millennial readers ... Google that if you didn't understand the reference) and tear out most of the pages.

Quit investing your life in go-nowhere relationships.

I'm giving you permission to date the girl you think is prettiest. You'll work harder to keep her. You'll spend your free time thinking about her. You'll find ways to make the other things work. And, if I'm her (scary visual, I'm aware), why would I want to leave someone who gives that kind of attention and/or affection?

Your client knows if you're interested or not. They know when your creative just isn't that creative. They know when there is a delay in response time. They know when you talk about "the policies" more than "the experience."

If you like tall girls or tall guys, go for it. If you're more of a sporty spice kind of guy, get you some.

And, if you work better with clients who have greater-than-average income, quit trying to sell your product at Wal-Mart. You, be you. Be the premium. Or be the bargain. But, in the name of Sam Hill, please make decisions which get you focused on *someone*, rather than *everyone*.

You'll never be happy. They'll never be happy. I'll never be happy. Gilmore will never be happy. (Too far? Maybe.)

Do not, and I repeat, DO NOT be afraid of declining business from a client if it is a distraction to what you should be doing – or *want to be doing*.

PERSONAL CONFESSION
___

Admittedly, it took quite a while to convince my therapist to let me share personal stories on this topic. Or, maybe it was just the fact that I had so many examples to share that they all blended into one, big shameful menagerie of regret. Honesty is healthy though, right? So, let's go.

Details aside, I remember a few relationships over the years where I had the "perfect girl." She was into me. Things were great ... on paper. No baggage. Attractive. College educated, employed, likely a 6-7 on the hot-crazy matrix. Things were good. Good, I reminded myself. This should be good.

But, WTF was wrong? Nothing. Sometimes, the relationship was so perfect that I wondered if *I* was even necessary. Hell, she was perfect in every way, but I just couldn't commit.

Enter stage left, train wreck of a not-as-attractive, recently-divorced, socially awkward single mom. Now you're speaking my language. What is wrong with me? Why would I want to make that trade?

Possible theories (as shared by various "experts" in my life who were always willing to freely offer unsolicited opinions):

- The "damaged" girl was more of a challenge.
- I liked being a "hero / savior" in relationships.
- The "perfect" girl was too intimidating.
- My family set a bad example of healthy marriages.
- Self-sabotage was just my "thing."

It took me a lot of years to accept that I really didn't give a rat's @ss what the reason was. I knew one thing: The one that fired my passion kept me coming back. The reason was irrelevant. And maybe it wouldn't work out in the end, but it was fun while it lasted. And if you love what you're doing, it never feels like work (get your mind out of the gutter).

Likewise, it took me even more years to draw the parallel between these truths and my professional life. Do what you love, with whom you love, and watch the rest work out. Often the "perfect" match isn't at all.

From the CEO's Desk

In a nearly perfect parallel, I recently found myself courting a potential client with the same kind of zeal with which I pursued that "not-as-attractive, recently-divorced, socially-awkward single mom." It was an identical parallel. This would-be client was a mess. Great business. Great revenue. Outstanding product. Trainwreck (like, you have no idea) of an operation - but with "potential" creeping out of every corner.

My rates were insulted. Our operation was insulted. Our ability to handle a business "their size" was questioned. (That one made me actually laugh.) In fact, I was even questioned about our recruiting practices of our staff. (Seriously, why is our recruiting any of your business?)

Yet, I found myself wanting so badly to play savior to this business owner. I wanted the product in my portfolio, obviously, but I wanted to be a hero this time. I knew what I could do with this brand and started living in my head, imagining the potential growth. I mean, when so much is wrong, it can only get better, right?

And, while I was out courting this chaos, I had that "perfect" client waiting to do business with me. The everything-is-just-right client was waiting for a proposal from me, but I was out of town trying to impress this other mess.

We made a deal. We started coordinating onboarding. I had email and text message commitments. My team started investing time. But the contract just kept getting ignored. We were expected to continue onboarding, but no signatures.

Then it happened, as expected.

"I just met someone else who I think is a better match for us."

While I would love to make this a lesson on integrity, I'll resist and solely focus on what I learned.

My lesson: You can't change people. I followed my passion to make the brand successful, but I can't save anyone. This client would have been a cancer to my business. Guaranteed. The one for which you make the greatest accommodations will be your greatest obstacle. I was about to reach and bend around every best practice we must make this one work, but I knew better.

I gracefully walked away (feeling a bit like a fool, honestly) and I don't regret a thing.

I know my type.

RYZE-ING TO THE OCCASION

I'd be lying if I told you that we haven't taken on some projects that we had no business being involved in – but lessons are often learned the hard way. The question to ask, of course, is when to cut bait. And, if you're smart, you cut sooner than later.

As recently as yesterday, I have been exchanging emails with a would-be client who has yet to sign a contract. We have already spent hours upon hours on the telephone (mostly, me helping them with advice on how to detangle themselves from a poorly managed deal with a prior distributor), but they have yet to pay anything or sign anything.

My radar has been on them for a while now, from the first engagement, but I have allowed the relationship to continue. There are flags all over this play, but I've continued to dialogue, as they are a referral from another business contact.

In quoting their projects, I offered as deep as a 50% discount on much of the work. (They are a non-profit, kind of, so I've been really generous, including many things we've just done *pro bono* already.)

Then came yesterday's email. I'll summarize.

"I've reviewed your fee schedule and it appears that you guys are making too much money on handling our account, so we're going to ask that you take a deeper discount."

My team had to take a step back at this point and really ask some tough questions. Their estimated monthly budget was $3,000. Yes. Only $3,000 / month. And they were offended because we were going to charge $500 / month to manage the account. I'll spare you the details as to what that entails, but suffice to say, it is pennies. It was the worst devaluing of my team that I have experienced in a long time – *and it felt gross*.

In a chapter about "Knowing Your Type," I give this illustration to give you permission to walk away. Red flags are red for a reason, and it isn't because they're romantic. One of the hardest things for an entrepreneur to do is to turn down business, but it is sometimes necessary.

At our agency, we use an exercise that we find quite useful when making these tough decisions. As we always have an active list of projects that are in the pipeline, we map out the next few months in advance, then ask the question about profitability. If we have more profitable work to keep everyone busy, we decline the low performer.

Remember, your goal is to do the *most profitable* and/or *most pleasurable* work. When you have the *option* to decline the low performers, you look at them a lot differently. If you don't have a date for the prom, you may go with the first person who asks. If three people ask, you get to pick.

We prefer to be the picker.

Today's Lessons Learned

- When you're good enough to attract multiple options, you have the power to choose, rather than settle.
- It is important to recognize your own personal *preferences*. Sometimes there is a natural attraction to a particular type of business or client. That's okay. Focus where you're happiest.
- Quit investing your time in go-nowhere relationships. Too many people need you, and would kill to have you, so stop spinning your wheels on the time-suckers.
- Never be devalued. Listen to me here. Never.

Now, Ask Yourself

- Self, do you spend enough time doing the things necessary to attract your would-be matches?
- Self, when you see people or situations which seem attractive, are you able to maintain objectivity, or do you dive in head-first?
- Self, have you spent sufficient time identifying your "type"? What do you like? Where do you thrive?
- Self, where were you happiest in your life? What can be done to focus more energy in that area?

On making a first impression.

CHAPTER 3: THE FIRST DATE
(part one)

Well, you made it. Clammy hands. Nervous energy. Wearing more *eau d 'toilet* than a reasonably-priced French call girl in the pale of the red lights. But you understand the value of first impressions now. Right? Make this count.

[insert dramatic record screeching noise]

Now, rewind 24 hours.

Assuming that this is a date that you've been anticipating for at least one week, you have likely engaged in the ceremonial first date preparations (to which we have all fallen prey). There's a science to it, after all.

Men:

1. The Haircut: Even if it is just a trim and shave, it mustn't be done at home. This requires some professional intervention. And, by haircut, I mean all the visibles, including those which may be protruding from the eyebrows, nose, and ears.

2. The Car Wash: Regardless of where you are going, even if you are meeting up somewhere, a guy always wants to have a clean car, inside and out. Just in case, make a good impression.

3. The Manscape: While only a first date, you can never be too

sure. (And, for the love of all things holy, if you don't know what this is, *please* look it up. She'll thank you.)

4. The Wardrobe: Stylish, but not too "metro." Coordinated, but not too planned. Something that says that you came to impress, but that you own more than one decent outfit. Gotta keep something for next time, eh?

5. The Pregame: Allow for 15 extra minutes in the shower (see #3). Shave to the perfect amount of five o'clock shadow (it's better to look like a man than a boy). Extra flossing. Maybe a few pushups. And then douse yourself in ungodly amounts of your favorite smelly things to highlight your Brut manliness.

Women (this list was written by a female colleague, so no man-bashing on my ignorance):

1. The Detailing: While guys may spend time detailing the car, women likely spend a week detailing themselves. Hair (cuts, roots, or full-on Dolly Partons), nails (fingers and toes), waxing (...), facial, and all the likely (or unlikely) rituals associated with "natural" beauty.

2. The Fashion Crisis: Assuming that she has not chosen the venue, the wardrobe crisis may be fatal. To heel, or not to heel? Jeans or a skirt? Sexy, but not slutty. Enough jewelry to accessorize, without being distracting. Oh, God, does this make my butt look fat? The girlfriend (either in person or on Facetime) critiquing every outfit.

3. The Hair / Makeup Redo: Once done, hair and makeup will likely not cooperate on the big day. Start over. Contemplate cutting off all your hair.

4. The Cancellation: While she may not actually cancel, this is always a step in the process which requires consideration. Yoga pants love you regardless.

5. The Time Lapse: While perfectly planned to the minute, assume you'll be late (but you're worth it, so he can wait ... and if he doesn't, he doesn't deserve you anyway). See step #4.

6. The Pregame: A glass of wine.

7. Repeat step #6.

8. Consider step #4 again.

9. The F#ck It: You've come this far; you might as well go. This is expensive makeup and you'll be damned if you're going to just wash it off and stay home now. He better be paying for dinner. Does he know how much this makeup costs?

10. Repeat step #6.

Tongue-in-cheek as these may seem, they are scientifically proven to be 97.1% accurate according to studies conducted by the *Society of Neurotic Dating Practices*. It's a thing. Look it up.

Maybe you offered a guilty laugh while reading those lists. And maybe they're a little exaggerated (although I find them to be remarkably accurate). But here is the ubiquitous truth: When planning a first impression, there is power in preparation.

Read that again.

When planning a first impression, there is power in preparation.

The first of anything is a monumental something. We remember firsts. First crushes. First kisses. First cars. They form an imprint on us – even a benchmark against which all subsequent encounters are measured. So, why not spend a little time to lather up the shaving cream and wear a little extra cologne? This is only going to happen once.

I speak to my staff all the time on the topic of job interviews (ironic, I know). We work in an industry that experiences high turnover, and due to the intellectual nature of our work, you can imagine that finding good help is hard. Add to that, since we work in the marketing industry, image matters. So, we are always looking for very smart people who present well and can autonomously add value. But, confession, it's about as easy as finding a unicorn giving CPR to a garden gnome on the sixth Thursday of the month.

Here's the thing about job interviews though: When I meet people at that first interview, I assume that I will never see that person look better than he /she does that day. I assume that this is the impression you've chosen to make to the world – after spending a little extra "first date" time getting ready.

The decision as to whether I am going to give this individual a full half-hour of my time is based solely on whether I believe that he or she even gave a rat's @ss to prepare for our meeting. Show up looking like you *gave* up and I will give up too. Show up looking like you took the time to impress, and I'm willing to invest about the same amount of time into our meeting.

And this isn't just about appearances, although that matters tremendously. I'm talking about the little things, like résumés. Don't you dare show up to a job interview without one and say something stupid like, "I was going to print that, but I forgot ... didn't have time ... ran out of paper ... the dog ate it ... whatever."

Translated: You're not valuable enough for me to prepare to meet you. Just like a first date, right?

HER: I'm so sorry I didn't brush my hair before this date, but I've been so busy.

I'll spare you his response.

But really, how is it different with our clients?

Regardless of the business you're in, you make first impressions every day. Every. Single. Day. Somebody walks into your store for the first time. Somebody calls your business for the first time. Somebody visits your website for the first time. Somebody visited your LinkedIn profile for the first time. Heck, somebody called inquiring about the open position you had posted and got a first impression of what it would be like to work at your place.

How did it go? Did you just scare away the unicorn and sacrifice the garden gnome on the altar of "too busy to prepare"?

If so, I say CHECK YOUR PRIORITIES.

Do not even attempt to convince me that you want – earnestly want – something better than you have right now while you're sitting there in sweatpants. If you can't iron your own clothes before a first date – a first impression – then don't waste even a moment of my time complaining about being single. You earned it. And if you can't proof your own résumé for typos, spare me the unemployment tears.

So, what's your ritual? If you don't have one, I want you to stop reading this book right now. I forbid you to continue reading until you get your sh#t together on this one.

If you don't know how to make a good first impression, you have no business making impressions at all – because you're making them, my friend. You're making them all the time and don't even know it. Hell, I had to make one on you to get you to even read this book (at least to chapter 3, I guess). I must have done something right, so maybe you should take my advice.

[HARD BREAK TO NEXT PAGE]

I hope you didn't just continue reading, flipping that page as if you had it all together, because that's just disappointing – and it is only you who stands to lose. And if you look straight in that mirror right now, that's not a loser looking back.

So, back to the question. What's your ritual? How do you prepare?

I remember giving dating advice to a friend of mine (interestingly, I was supposed to be having dinner with him tonight, but he stood me up, so I'm here writing this chapter instead). He was all into this girl and didn't know if she was into him too.

He finally got up the gall to ask her to go to dinner, but he wasn't sure if she understood his intentions. As they belonged to a mutual social circle, there was a possibility that she thought they were just having dinner as friends. Nearly paralyzed with fear, he panicked. How would he know? How would he ask? What would he say? How awkward would that be if she wasn't on the same page?

My advice: "Stop. Trust me, you will know. You've seen her a hundred times before at various events and gatherings. You know what she normally looks like, so you'll know if she looks different tonight. Based on how prepared she is, you'll know her intentions."

I saw him the next day and I think he was still in shock a bit.

Him: "That dress. That yellow dress. Her hair. Some perfume I've never smelled."

Yeah, she was prepared. She went through her ritual, and it worked. He was smitten.

If you're in a business like mine (advertising and marketing, if you haven't been keeping up), we are forever standing in front of clients who know exponentially more about their businesses than we ever could. Yet, they call us for advice on how to sell their product or even brand themselves in the marketplace.

Our ritual: Research.

If I am going to go stand in front of a client who has spent his or her career in a specific industry and talk about how they need to change the way they do business, I would be a fool to not prepare.

Have you ever seen the movie *What Women Want*, with Mel Gibson and Helen Hunt? I love that movie. Remember the scene where Nick Marshall (Gibson) was presented with the task of explaining how to sell products which were predominantly sold to women? He went home and waxed his legs. He gave himself a facial. He put on pantyhose. And, as hilarious as the scene was, it was a perfect example of preparation at its finest. He cared enough to be ready for the next step.

But maybe you work in retail. Or an attorney's office. Or you're still a student. What is your first date preparation?

The reality of this chapter is that the details of your vocation or livelihood don't matter. What matters is that you're spending the necessary time *every day* to prepare yourself for an *entire day* of first impressions. New clients. New employees. New prospects. New vendors. They all meet you for the first time at some point.

What are they remembering?

And, more importantly, would they go out with you again?

PERSONAL CONFESSION
___

Recently, I visited an office supply store looking for a special type of paper. Usually, I would have someone just order office supplies online, but for this project, I wanted to touch it myself and see what kind of impression it made. (I was so concerned about the first impression that I took the time to visit the Office Depot myself ... oops, I just said their name.)

I entered the store and asked the nearest salesperson if he was available to assist me. He let me know that he was involved in another project. Noted.

I continued looking through the aisles of paper until I spotted another young lady. Same question. She wasn't able to do much in the way of communicating, so she found a third person to help her translate from English to English (yes, you read that right).

I was shocked when person number three quickly let me know that the Office Depot does not carry the paper I was looking for – because I was asking for a special size. (They have cutting service, by the way.)

While I likely reacted more with my face than my words, it did catch the attention of a fourth individual who got involved. I believe she realized that she wasn't going to convince me to leave them alone, so she radioed in for backup (you read that correctly too). The store manager proceeded to handle the situation exclusively by speaking to her on a radio from across the room.

After several relays on this radio about how the paper cutter was broken, with constant emphasis on how it wasn't their fault, the store manager walked his Claus-like physique to the paper section and asked what the problem was.

The *problem*. I was "the problem," so said their verbiage.

I'll spare you the details of our exchange, noting that I did end up leaving the store with the paper I wanted in the size I needed. And, during the final minutes of our conversation, the store manager attempted to make light of the "confusion."

Damage done. There were no confusions. There was just terrible service.

While all five of these office supply connoisseurs showed up to work just another shift, I showed up for the first time. See what happened there?

Not only have they lost my business, but now I am successfully sharing my story with the millions upon millions of people reading this book – many of whom may live in Coral Springs, Florida near University Road.

Honest question: What kind of first impression are you making?

"Dress for the job you want," they say. How are you preparing?

From the CEO's Desk

In a past life, I worked in the industry of post-secondary education. Yes, the industry. It's a business, like it or not. And the saddest part about most people who work in education is that they don't see it as an industry. No offense to educators; I'm one of you. But *I* realize that everything is tied to a transaction. Sorry.

And, while in the classroom, I would *always* teach my students how to tie *value* to every interaction. Value equals job security and advancement... one hundred percent of the time. Don't believe me? I'll take your job.

Well, once, while visiting a campus located in Jersey City, New Jersey, I was faced with a unique challenge. In the aftershock of Hurricane Sandy, students in our nursing and medical-related programs were struggling to get employment throughout Manhattan and east-coast New Jersey. Most of them were doing their internships when the hurricane struck the area and battered the entire region. Many of the clinics and medical offices shut down entirely, but others were struggling to even reopen due to the damage, and our internship team was struggling to keep students engaged. The medical offices hosting these interns became much more selective about who they wanted in their offices, as they had little to no time to supervise bad behavior. Fearing dropouts and other program flight risks, internship team asked me to get involved. (I'm laughing right now recalling the story.)

"I'd be happy to help," I enthusiastically agreed. "Please set up a mandatory meeting at 3:00pm on Thursday and only invite your worst students. The others don't need to be there."

Fast forward to Thursday.

I entered the assigned meeting room at about 3:10pm. (I wanted all the students to be annoyed at my tardiness before I got there. It was a mandatory meeting, after all, and I was late. How dare I!)

"Good afternoon! How is everyone doing today? Thank you for being here for this *invitation only* meeting. I asked your internship coordinators to only invite the worst students today, and *you* made the cut. Congratulations!"

Intercity school meeting of the worst college students on campus … enter Mr. White Ass who starts the meeting by insulting everyone. Nobody in that room was comfortable – staff included. Well, except me. I knew where I was going with it. Why? Because I prepare.

"My understanding is that each of you in this room is actively on internship right now. I further understand that not even one of your internship supervisors have expressed any interest in hiring you when your internship ends. Looking around this room, I can't say that I blame them."

The looks.

Girl in front row pipes up. "I wouldn't want to work there even if they offered me a job!"

"Really?" I added with a faux gasp and concerned visage. "It must be terrible there. What is happening?!"

"They're terrible to their people. There is this one lady who just criticizes everything I do."

"What is her role there? She sounds horrible."

"It's Dr. Alvarez. She's the site manager."

"Wait! You mean to tell me that this woman ... Dr. Alvarez, I think you said ... feels that she could possibly teach anything to an intern? That's preposterous!" My pantomime must have been outrageous because half of the class started laughing.

My plan was working.

"Perhaps," I continued, "there is value to listening to her input. She clearly knows a thing or two, else she wouldn't be a doctor – and wouldn't be the practice manager. Ever thought of asking for her help before she volunteers it? You may earn an ally – and a job."

"Well, if she was paying me …"

I interrupted, "… then you would brush your hair?"

"Laughing wrinkle pants" in the back row belly laughs at his classmate getting schooled.

"I'm sorry, is this funny?" I *politely* asked.

"Well, yeah. She thinks she already knows everything. That's dumb."

"Dumb?" I asked. "Is it any dumber than showing up to work looking like you woke up in the bottom of a hamper?"

The rest of the class laughed. Here we go.

Once my platform was established, the conversation was incredible from that point forward. They respected the boldness that it took to confront them with the tough conversations. We had an hour together and we had some *hard* talks about the value of first impressions. Wrinkled uniforms. Hair that doesn't even looked brushed. In some cases, it is just the defeated attitude that the students carried with them.

Our conversation was outstanding that day, and each student took the time to shake my hand on the way out the door, promising to "clean it up" while they were out on site.

"Every time you speak to a new person, you are making a first impression. Use it. Even if you screw it up, you get to do it again tomorrow with someone else. Don't waste that. Look like the brand you want to portray. Act it."

You know what's wrong with today's generation (truly spoken like an old man)? Nobody takes the time to tell them about life and how to succeed. We're too busy worrying about offending someone and sparing their feelings. But, I've learned, young people want guidance. They want to know how to get ahead. They want to hear it straight.

Best class I ever had the chance to challenge.

Ryze-ing to the Occasion

First impressions are so complicated, aren't they? You get one shot, and only one shot. After that, you're trying to overcome a bad impression – no matter what people tell you about being able to recover.

Here at Ryze Agency, we're no exception. And it is stressful.

I'd love to tell you that we get it right every time, but I'd be flat out lying. We're human, after all. But we try. And that's what matters.

In a digital world, where Zoom has become more common than handshakes, our goal is face-to-face, knees-to-knees interaction – in person.

Too many companies rely on email and asynchronous communication as being the go-to style. Not here. We believe in relationships, and relationships are not built over Zoom calls. They can be nurtured, but Zoom is a terrible place to make a first impression.

One of my professional goals has always been *being present*. Repeat that: "Being present." When your client sees that you are willing to get on an airplane and travel to their office for a meeting that *could have* been done on a phone call, there is a heightened level of respect for your time. They see the value you place on them. They see that you are about relationship, and not merely about transactions. They see your investment (and human nature is to return favors, after all).

Be present.

Today's Lessons Learned

- When planning a first impression, there is power in preparation.
- First impressions are permanent.
- You have 100% control of the image that you portray to the world. The question is not "if" you can make a good impression; it is "how much work are you going to put into trying."
- Every day, take the necessary time to prepare yourself for an *entire day* of first impressions.

Now, Ask Yourself

- Self, when is the last time that you were *intentional* about the impression you were about to make? Was it successful?
- Self, what is your ritual when preparing for a first encounter? Do you even have one?
- Self, other than the way you dress and groom, what other ways are you and your business making first impressions today?
- Self, what one action item can you implement today to improve your image?

On learning to provide value.

Chapter 4: The First Date
(part deux)

So important that it gets two chapters, we're continuing to talk about first dates. Why wouldn't we? So far, we've only gotten to the point that you walked in the door and didn't look like you just got sideswiped by a train. She saw you from across the room and agreed to stay for dinner, but now you must open your mouth and form words at some point.

Oh, my sweet Lord, how this can go so wrong!

Most folks prefer to have a dinner date as their first time together. Others are into this new "coffee and bagels" thing, but I think that's just a lame way of escaping interrogation-like torture in under an hour (assuming that the other person didn't read the last chapter). Coffee can be five minutes or three hours, all without pissing off the server for holding up the table.

Personally, I'm a fan of the dress up and go to dinner kind of date. I want to see how much time she took to impress me. Call me shallow, but it is kind of a raw read on how interested she is. Trust me, fellas, if she's interested, you'll know it.

The point of this chapter, however, isn't to repeat the last one. It is to talk about what happens once the first look is over. And, as a wise man once wrote: "Charm lasts about fifteen minutes."

First impressions made. He's into you. She's clearly interested. The client is willing to talk. Whatever.

Now what?

Now you better have some substance, because up until now, you've been all curb appeal. If nothing meaningful happens when your pie hole opens, this has just been a waste of everyone's time – yours included.

Everyone is done ogling each other and sniffing to identify the price tag of the elixir of choice. Now conversation begins.

Nine out of ten experts agree that there are two rules that you must strongly obey at this point of the game:

- RULE #1: Find common ground.
- RULE #2: Create intrigue.

Likely, you already know something about your dinner mate, else you wouldn't be there in the first place. Also likely, something has gotten your attention after the visual stimulus wore off. (And, if you know *nothing* about her prior to dinner, kudos to you, young buck. Go get 'em.)

Common ground is typically easy to find. I mean, everyone likes pizza and puppies. But there must be something more. Find it. Quickly.

Travel? Safe. Sports? Safe. Music? Safe.

Politics? Religion? Daddy issues? MAY DAY!

And this next point cannot be emphasized enough: *There is no need to bare all on the first date.* Keep it interesting and comfortable, without giving up all your hidden corners. Touch on some basics. Showcase your finest qualities. Tell some funny stories.

It's called building rapport. And it is the point of this entire chapter.

The goal of this date isn't to buy a ring. The goal of the first date is to get a second date – assuming your would-be beau meets all the early criteria for an LTR ("long-term relationship," for those of you who are still catching up).

Too often, folks are so much into efficiency that they completely miss out on the best stage of the game. Creating the intrigue is what makes flirting fun. There is a certain kind of mystery that can only exist in the subtly of early attraction.

Think about the best first date you ever had. Was it great because you learned everything about her at the first meeting? Likely not. To the contrary, what made it fun was the journey of discovery. And, with each date, the more you learned, the more you realized there was so much more that you didn't even know yet.

Sadly, not every date goes so well and both Rule #1 and Rule #2 get trampled like a cheap rug, but there are early signs of a rogue dater. For the sake of newbies to this game, let's classify a bit.

- The Verbal Vomit Dude: Y'all know the type. You're sitting there at dinner and suddenly you realize that you know far too much about a total stranger. You've attempted to find common ground, but he's not interested in hearing about your story; he's more interested in making sure that you know everything there is to know about him. From childhood to present day, there is hardly a moment you've missed, illustrated in perfect detail.

- The Boundary Maker: Ah, yes. There she is. Sitting across the table, but she might as well be sitting across the room. You wonder why she is even here tonight, really. Fearful about giving up too much information on a first date, she keeps you at a remote distance while deciding the fate of your second date.

- The Resume Reader: In a would-be attempt at "sharing," this name dropper spends all his time feeding you some embellished highlight reel which bears about as much resemblance to reality as cauliflower pizza. Although he may be sharing freely, you walk away feeling like you know nothing about this person. It's a game of who did more and knows more famous people. Like you got slapped into the middle of a game show and the only thing missing is a Chuck Woolery segue (by the way, I know him, if we're name dropping).

Now, think about the salesperson who hard closes on the first visit to the car dealership. Now think about the salesman who stays in contact with you after your visit and remembers your face when you show up on the showroom floor again.

Sell yourself, but not out of desperation. Let the relationship blossom and organically bloom.

[hard cut]

So, you're at your first meeting with your client. You're all dressed up and ready to go, but you've only got until midnight here, Cinderella. Time is ticking. What's your focus?

What is most important to share first? Preparation, remember? In the elevator speech of life, what needs to be said now? And what can wait until next time?

Remember, the goal is to *get to* "next time." That's the only goal today.

Does the client need a guided tour through your entire catalog? Do they need a full history of the company and its staff, including full résumés and "favorite past times," as listed on several company websites? Do they need to listen to your full explanation of the return policy?

No. No. And another emphatic NO.

The client, just like your first date, needs to know enough to know they want to see you again. Most people don't want to know everything about you. They want to know the things they like. Cater to that. If I walked into the Wal-Mart to buy a pair of jeans (please note that I would *never* do this), I wouldn't appreciate the clerk taking me up to home drapery because "it is important to know all of what Wal-Mart has to offer."

No, it isn't. If I am in the market for $20 jeans, let me buy them. Be the best $20 jean company in my zip code ... and shut up. And if we get to know each other during that transaction, feel free to mention the drapes, if you think I have interest. But not every person is going to have interest in everything you have to offer.

AND THAT'S OKAY.

Be okay with that.

Are you okay with that?

This point can seem contrary to a lot of pop culture advice so I don't want this to be glossed over. Too many "experts" give the advice that you should always be selling, so long as you have the client's attention. And, while I agree that you should be selling, I want to make this point painfully clear: *You should be selling the relationship; not the product.* There is nothing your business offers that is more important to your client than a healthy, committed relationship with you. Whether you are an entrepreneur or work on the sales team of a Fortune 500, your clients are buying YOU. People, myself included, will sacrifice product quality for outstanding service.

Watch me prove my point.

I have an uncle who was recently diagnosed with pancreatic cancer. Certainly, that's not the best news you could get, but I have to tell you that I was fascinated hearing about his selection process while choosing a treatment center. He's a man of means, so his options were pretty good. He can afford to get treatment outside of his insurance network, so he can handpick his doctors if he chooses to. A nice position to be in, for sure, but when he and my aunt were flying from state to state to interview physicians and treatment centers, he declined some of the biggest names in cancer research ... because of the lack of connection he felt to the doctor.

One was too unsympathetic. One was too calloused. He felt that one was intimidated by him asking so many questions. One wanted to direct withdrawal access to his bank account so they could collect their payments electronically. It felt like he was never going to decide.

Hear me here: A man with a life-threatening condition was willing to pass on some of the best physicians in the land, simply because he didn't think they cared enough about him. It was personal. It was relational. It was everything you wouldn't expect.

Logic would dictate that he should choose the physician with the greatest survival rate. Or the guy who has the most experience with his specific type of cancer. But his criteria were all about the relationship. With a blank check, he decided with emotion.

How many of us are guilty of the same thing though? We buy things because of the feelings they give us. We buy from people because of the attention they give us. We appreciate the beautician who is willing to come in on her day off. We love the car dealer who knows our names when we walk in the door. We want the personalized service. The commitment. The comfort that longevity brings.

And, if we're going to take this a step further, that relationship keeps things together when things go wrong – and something always goes wrong. The relationship creates a bond that is difficult for circumstances to sever.

Back to that first date though, focus on the highlight reel.

What is it that you hope to get out of today's interaction (Rule #1: Find common ground)? And, now, how can I get you to come back next time (Rule #2: Create intrigue)?

In the d? ng scene, you know exactly how to do this already - intuitively, I would argue.

While talking about travel, the topic of tasty food enters the conversation. You talk about this off-the-beaten-path seafood joint that has the freshest crab legs. BAM! You have a second date.

While talking to your client, you find out that they have a need for another service (one you don't offer). You offer to set up a referral call with an associate who you would recommend in the industry. BAM! You have a reason to meet again.

It's the same thing.

I own a few businesses, some larger than others. But, when engaging a new potential client, I make a point of always figuring out which SINGLE business is best suitable to start the conversation. I carry various business cards, in fact.

A staff member of mine once asked me, "Aren't you going to talk to them about _____ too?" It was a valid question. I explained to him that my priority was to be relevant to the client in ONE way first. Once I'm in the door and the relationship is blooming, I can *now* discuss other ways that we can connect. The priority, of course, is knowing how we have help them now.

Think about this illustration.

You're at a restaurant, casually engaging in conversation with a friend (or even that first date) and the server approaches the table.

You assume that she is going to ask you for your drink order, right? And you assume that because most *good* servers understand how to pace a meal. Why? Because they know that an enjoyable experience leads to a bigger tip. And, the longer you sit there, the more likely you are to order more drinks. And the more drinks you consume before you order, the more reckless you are with your order.

Now, imagine she approaches the table, and the conversation goes something like this:

"Hi, I'm Susie. I'll be your server today. Do you have any questions about the menu?" Assuming you don't, she continues, "Great. What can I get you to drink? And an appetizer? And your entrée? Soup or salad? Great, and what would you like for dessert?"

Quite the first visit to the table, eh?

There is a reason why restaurants put the dessert menu on a different piece of paper: They want you to enjoy the meal first. The appetizers will give you an idea of what the meal will taste like. And, once finished with an enjoyable meal, it's a lot easier to sell dessert.

Make this engagement last longer. Foreplay is necessary in this game. Don't be greedy. Follow me, chief?

So how are you preparing?

How are you learning enough about your client to know what they want or need from you most? They don't need everything – and certainly not at once, so what are you doing to learn?

Do you prepare differently for different lead sources? (Compare this to how the conversation changes when you're on a date with a "set up" rather than an online meeting.)

Do you know what your best qualities even are? Do you value things about you or your company that the rest of the world just doesn't value? (Your intrigue with forestry isn't likely an intrigue she shares.)

And, for God's sake, know when to cut the bait. Remember, you're not only selling; you're also a buyer.

Back to the dating comparison, you want to make yourself a valuable commodity in the great social exchange, but you also want to feel like the other person is bringing an equal or greater value.

To that point, how are you screening your clients? You're not the fit for everyone, no matter how much you'd like to think so. What are your "must haves" and "can't stands"?

Draw the line somewhere.

> **CONFESSION**: It physically hurts me to write this (especially considering that I am writing this on an airplane while sitting next to our director of accounts), but I am *terrible* at drawing the line. Terrible. Like, Shift-F7 doesn't have enough RAM to explain to you how bad I am at this.

I'd like to believe that it's because I just see the best in everyone (insert sunshine and rainbows), but I'm not that nice of a person. Perhaps I just think that I can fix anything? Or maybe I just like saving the day?

Regardless, I spend more time dealing with some of the most ridiculous projects than I would care to admit. And, as you could predict, they are the ones who monopolize my time.

You're familiar with the 80/20 rule, right? With tons of applications, I'll illustrate this point by saying that I spend 80% of my time dealing with 20% of my clients. In fact, I'd argue to say that these clients likely make up less than 20% of my annual revenue. The ROI on my time is awful, but I'm just a giver, I guess (or a fool).

And, back to that first date. Face it. You know. You know if it is going somewhere. The ROI on a first date should be calculated, I would argue. I don't get that many nights to spend on dinner dates and movies, so why would I want to spend them with someone with whom I don't see a future. I would be better setting a *first* date with a different person than sticking around here for a round two with *Vanilla Wafers*.

My time, and your time, is too valuable.

Draw the line.

Once you've done your job establishing why he or she should want YOU, now you get to choose.

Same with a client, no? Sell that relationship (yourself). Once he's intrigued, now you get to ask the questions. Play a little hard to get now. Don't put it all out there.

(And, if you're really clever, you'll know exactly how to keep them guessing.)

Personal Confession

I remember going out on this date years back. I knew this girl socially but didn't know much about her other than that she was cute and really funny.

Anyway, we went out to dinner first, then we were going to go to some nearby dessert and cigar bar (strange combo, but it worked). They played live music, but mellow enough that you could enjoy a conversation.

First date, I learned that she couldn't drink alcohol because of her sobriety commitment through AA. She couldn't even drink water with her meal, because she had bariatric surgery a few years back, so she could only eat small quantities at a time – and no sugar. I learned that she was divorced, because she cheated on her ex-husband (part of her party days). I learned that she was paying back a series of bad checks she had written in the past and was settling out of court. I learned that she lived in an apartment, because she had recently filed bankruptcy due to financial issues.

Oh, I learned *so* much that night.

While we had a good laugh over it, I can't tell you that I was primed for a second date. I felt like she had already removed any ounce of mystery and "getting to know you" that could be in store for round two.

From the CEO's Desk

A client of ours – the "big name" kind – has been dragging its feet for months and months (nearly 18 of them). We have done everything right. We have overdelivered on every promise, met every deadline, and then waited ridiculous amounts of time to get paid. Classic.

Yet, I've never disconnected from them. Maybe this goes back to my superlative inability to draw lines, but I'd like to think this one is more calculated.

They have hired everyone in town to do work that we have offered to do. They have rebuffed our marketing strategies, only to go fail on their own – time and time again. It is such a strange relationship.

Well, amid them dodging phone calls and attempting to dishonor signed contracts, our firm knocked it out of the park on a project for another client. Like, KILLED IT kind of win. #tigerblood

You won't be surprised when I tell you that I ensured that they found out - quickly. And in detail. And with a little *Whoop Ass*™ sprinkled on top.

The CEO of their company received a personalized message from a mutual contact which was polite, yet practically custom-written to rub noses in the smeared defecation known as our relationship. It wasn't 45 seconds later that he reached out to talk.

The theme of the conversation: "If you can do it for them, you can do it for us."

Yeah, champ, that has been the conversation for the last 18 months, but you've dismissed all of our *free* advice. Maybe if I charged more ...

The point, of course, is that drawing lines can be healthy. We didn't sit around trying to win their business. In fact, in a conversation not weeks prior to this whole reemergence of interest, I let them know that we would prefer to not continue our relationship, as their business was just not worth our time. We drew the line.

Like the ex who sees you about town with the new flame, interest peaks and the whole game changes. Just like that.

Be in control.

(For the record, they wired us the entire past due amount the same day, as I refused to reengage without it.)

Ryze-ing to the Occasion

Not everyone is meant to work on every project. Not everyone is compatible with every client. Not everyone "gets the joke," in some cases. And this is critical to understand as your team expands.

Personality is as much a part of success as knowledge. Likes, dislikes, and personal preferences are every bit as important as skill when it comes to successfully working with a client.

We have this situation arise on a regular basis. And, while our business model may be different from yours, it is essential that we match projects to personalities. In the advertising world, we do our best to even match demographics to projects (like having a woman lead the project on a product whose consumer is female, and other such matches).

Traditionally, like at a restaurant or a call center, the next client/project gets assigned to the next available server or customer service agent. It is more efficient, for sure, but is it as effective? I'd argue not.

When new clients come on board, our first go-to strategy is to offer up the client/project to the team and see who shows an interest. Not only do you get higher job satisfaction, but you get more passionate work from your people. If they love the project, they work harder.

Recently, we engaged in a new project for a client who sells some "off-color" personal care products. The products are incredible, honestly, in terms of quality. And the only thing better than the products themselves is the personality of the brand. (If you're curious, check them out at www.wtfnovelties.com. And realize that I have never given you the name of another client in this book, so this one must be special.)

If you looked at that website, you'll understand my point. Not everyone would be successful on that project. Some staff members, I would confess, were offended by the project. They grew uncomfortable even talking about it during staff meetings.

Rather than assign the project to the next available artist, we chose the artist who best fit the project. He was perfect for it (more than we even realized when he was assigned). In fact, so much so that I think I have lost all respect for him. (He knows I'm joking.)

Find a match. Match your staff to your clients and everyone will be happier for it.

Today's Lessons Learned

- The goal of a first date is to get a second date. Nothing more. Think "intrigue."
- Relationships are built on common ground. Find similarities fast and stay in that lane.
- Always have an elevator speech prepared. It is part of your personal branding.
- Create intrigue.

Now, Ask Yourself

- Self, when you meet new people, do you have a goal in mind (like a second date) or do you just seem to aimlessly go with the flow?
- Self, do you open up too fast when you meet new people? Too slowly? How do you find balance to keep the intrigue?
- Self, what is it about you that people find the most interesting? How do you highlight that part about yourself?
- Self, would you want to meet you twice?

NOT A CHAPTER, BUT A GOOD LIFE LESSON
WRITING YOUR ELEVATOR SPEECH

I used to be the head of the public speaking department at a university near my hometown. (Honestly, one of the best gigs I have ever had. I got to watch people *become*. And if you don't know what I mean, just move on. It isn't important enough to the lesson to dwell here.)

I was forever fascinated that each time I would teach an introductory course on public speaking, the hardest assignment for the entire class was writing a 2-minute elevator speech.

In context, let's realize that I'm asking a person to speak for 120 seconds about the one thing in the world on which he or she is the world's foremost authority. It would seem as if 120 seconds would barely skim the surface of their knowledge. Yet, without fail, this was the hardest assignment of the semester. Every. Single. Time.

Like, let's be serious here. Who knows more about you than you?

I've heard excuses for days. Some folks excused themselves by saying that they just didn't know what someone would want to hear. Some claimed low self-esteem. Some objected on the grounds of privacy. My favorite, of course, was that student who simply didn't want to share all his accomplishments for fear that he would sound like he was bragging. My advice: "My dad always said that it isn't bragging if it's true."

All those things may be true, but none of them help us get to the point of the tutorial. Being able to speak about yourself is the only way to sell yourself. Being able to speak about yourself is the only way to sell your brand. Being able to speak about yourself is the only way to have a successful relationship. Being able to speak about yourself is the only way to hear how ridiculous you sound when you speak about yourself. (Try it in a mirror some time. One of the most painful experiences you will ever have. And one of the most eye-opening.)

So now let's talk about you.

I want to ask you five questions about yourself. And I want you to be able to answer each of them in 150 words. No more. No less. I'm giving you an outline to write your 750-word elevator speech.

> NOTE: You should have several versions of this because every single facet of your life should be explained uniquely. Don't be the person on a job interview talking about how much she loves puppies (unless you're applying for a job as a dog walker).

> YOUR MISSION: Decide what it is you're hoping to accomplish with this introduction. Most people will just start to ramble and not stay on topic. With an elevator speech, my friend, not only do you get to choose the topic ... you ARE the topic. Ask yourself, "If this introduction goes exactly as planned, what would I like to happen because of it?" It could be getting a job. It could be getting a date. It could be getting a potential client to sign a contract. First, start with the goal, then reverse engineer the conversation. After all, you're in charge – for two minutes anyway. Ready? Set. Impress.

> SCENARIO: I am meeting a well-published author for the first time and want her opinion on my upcoming book. Ideally, I would love for her to write a foreword.

QUESTION ONE: What one relevant fact would a person want to know about you and how does it relate to what you're trying to accomplish today? Be sure that your fact is rooted on common ground with the other person.

Good afternoon, Jane. I'm Mark Young. It is so nice to meet you today, as I think we have some things in common. I've been a fan of yours for quite a while and loved your book back in 2010. In fact, I'm in the process of writing a book myself right now and would love it if you could give me some tips on how you were able to accomplish everything you have.

My book falls in the same categories as yours: business, self-help, and entrepreneurship. It's a passion of mine, so I find it super easy to write about, but I'm always looking for expert opinions on its relatability to the public. Sometimes it's hard to gauge, as everyone in my circle is very complimentary. They all like me though, so who knows if they're being honest? I need more people to not like me, I guess.

QUESTION TWO: Why does this person want to help you? What does the other person gain by helping you?

It's important to me to garner the opinions of well-respected people in this field prior to taking the title to publication and I would really love it if I could get your input. I was reading an article about you recently and it said that you frequently work with student writers to help them hone their craft. If you're up for taking on a guy who is a little bit older than most of your students, I would love to seek your advice – either now, or at a time that works better for you. Certainly, your time is more valuable than I could possibly afford to pay, but I would love to have your input, even if it meant asking you if you would write a foreword to the book itself.

QUESTION THREE: What have you done to establish yourself as a person of credibility? Why would this person want to continue engaging past this dialogue? Like attracts like, so you must somehow match your audience.

It may sound crazy to be so brazen and ask this at a first meeting, but I may never get this chance again, so I'm taking a chance. That's what

I have learned from my years in business, and, coincidentally, one of the topics that I write about in my book. I have had a lot of chances to fail in my life, but the times that I have succeeded have all been the result of my relentless pursuit toward "YES." That's just how I live. Everything with purpose.

Yes, I have been a business owner and marketer for many years. Yes, I have been a college professor for nearly the same number of years. Yes, I have a lot of college degrees and initials behind my name. But the only reason any of those things happened was because I was willing to say YES - even when it was scary.

QUESTION FOUR: What is the most important thing you want this person to know about you right now? There must be a takeaway.

Overall, I think I count myself as successful. I've done a lot of different things in life, which have led me to where I am now, and I really want to use my experiences to benefit others. I've learned a lot of lessons the hard way, and I think that having the ability to be a storyteller is a unique gift. If I can use this gift, combined with my experiences as an entrepreneur, I'm convinced that I can save some people the trouble that I had getting started in the world.

I didn't have an easy time in my early years, but I am grateful for the lessons I learned, both the hard way and through the many amazing mentors I have had. I want to be that mentor, if only through the written word, to others and help them mature faster than I did.

QUESTION FIVE: What do you want from the person (again)? What are the next steps that anyone must take?

I know I mentioned this before, but if you would help mentor me the way I want to mentor others, which would be an honor like no other, given my respect for you. You have something I need, and my impression is that you are the type of person who enjoys helping others reach their goals.

So, do you mind if we can somehow keep in touch? I'm serious about the foreword to my book too. That would be such an honor to have you do that.

And, if I haven't said it yet, thank you so much for listening to my story. It means so much to have gotten this much of your time.

By positioning yourself *before* the meeting, you will be able to remember these few "anchors" to the conversation. Ad lib as necessary, but stick to the outline. That's the goal. Create an outline of your major points and stick to it throughout.

The same holds true for job interviews.

The same holds true for dating. Think about what you are willing to share ahead of time, then feel the moment. Having a plan helps you make good decisions.

And the same holds true when courting clients. Know what you're there to do. Nothing is worse than being a business owner who agrees to a meeting with a vendor, only to have the person ramble on with no content to the conversation. I'd rather buy from someone else on principle in that case.

On having substance.

Chapter 5: When Minute 16 Matters Most

(Subtitled: IQ Is In)

So, here's the deal, Sparky: Charm only works for about 15 minutes. Like it or leave it, it's the worst truth bomb I could possibly share with you 16 minutes after you started to make a first impression. And, just in case you hadn't gotten this memo: Life isn't fair, and everyone is blessed with a different IQ score. (*Very* different.)

Here's another fun fact for you: 85% of the US population believes that they have above average intelligence.

I'll leave you alone for a minute to ponder that one.

There yet?

Another minute?

Let me help break that down for you, maybe.

Eighty-five percent of the population believes they have above average IQ. Now, the statistics on this are alarming, honestly. And, while I will assume that anyone reading this book is in the "above average" demographic [wink, wink], the truth is that there are a lot of people out there who really think they have it all together (and are talking about how the rest of us are stupid).

You may need another minute with that one.

Somewhere in the world, someone with an IQ significantly lower than the current temperature in your living room is talking about how *you* are stupid (which we know isn't true, because you are reading this book, proving both your superior IQ and discerning taste).

> **CONFESSION:** I laughed writing that last sentence. It was actually half laugh and half chortle. Why a chortle, you ask? Simply to demonstrate my above average vocabulary and secure my place in the upper end of our statistical anomaly.

Back to business.

Remember, 85% of the population believes that they have above average IQ, meaning that, by mere definition, 35% of them are wrong. And, in my best big brother kind of way, I give you this advice: DON'T BE ONE OF THOSE PEOPLE.

So, why the talk about IQ? Well, journey with me to the restaurant of your choice.

Date night. Table for two. You spot her across the room as you enter the restaurant. You're not one for blind dates, but there she sits, alone, waiting for you to arrive. Stunning. You thank heaven, earth, and anyone else listening. (Insert chorus of angels.)

You get the point.

You introduce yourself. Sit down. Pray to Zeus that things go according to your recently-devised, post-first-glance plans.

The initial conversation flows, touching on the usual topics:

- Sorry, I'm late. There was traffic (as if she, also, didn't have

- to drive there, Sherlock).
- Did you have a tough time finding the restaurant?
- You look nice tonight. You're even more stunning than _____ described you.

Yadda, yadda, yadda (thanks, Seinfeld, that phrase has been stuck in my head for over twenty years now).

You order a bottle of wine. You order your meals. You're a half hour into this event and realize that there is, literally, no substance to this conversation. We're talking about calamari and merlot. And, while the scenery is nice, this isn't going anywhere right now.

She excuses herself to the ladies' room and you sit there asking yourself this one important question: "What in the world did we just talk about?"

Nothing.

She's all curb appeal, but nothing is going on past the front door. If it weren't for your intrinsic interest in the packaging, there was really nothing of value in the box.

Sure, she's probably a nice person, but she just lacks ... well, lacks. I'll just leave it right there.

She returns and asks, "Now, where did we leave off?"

You, honestly, don't know.

And, perhaps, she thinks you guys have had a great conversation.

Been there?

Ladies, feel free to replace the pretty girl story with a handsome, well-dressed man who can't get past video games and football. You'll feel our pain.

So, why does it matter?

Because charm only lasts for about 15 minutes, after which you better know what you're talking about – because your clients can see right through you.

You Can't Make This Stuff Up

Recently, we had hired a new employee at our organization. He had been here for a week and came with some extensive experience (as he kept reminding us). He was a social media manager who "was recruited to and graduated from the first university in the country with a social media program."

After a week at the firm, he was to have completed an in-depth dive into the social media strategies of one of our clients. His choice. One.

The time came for his presentation to management. He came to my office to present and started to get a bit uncomfortable. When asked why, he said that he expected to have the conference room, with an overhead projector and laser pointer and ... blah, blah, blah.

"I don't need a fireworks show." I assured him. "Just walk us through what you've found."

He opened his PowerPoint presentation and began to walk us through his numbers. Then he got noticeably nervous when, three slides in, I pulled up the same data from our actual social media platforms and none of the numbers matched.

He fumbled.

I pointed out the variance in the numbers, full well giving him sufficient space to explain the gap.

"Well, I ran these numbers the other day," he defended. "The numbers could have gone up since then."

Gone up? But the live data is *lower* than the data he was showing me.

I'll spare you the details, but suffice to say that it was a mess. Without the fireworks show, he didn't know how to impress anyone. He was all about the pomp and the circumstance, but none of the content. I felt bad for the guy, and even offered to give him a second chance to redo his work and bring it back to us the following Monday. I felt *that* bad. Like, a total opportunity for a redo.

Funny ending to this story: He agreed that he would take the weekend to put together a presentation that made sense, then walked immediately to his office, packed his personal effects, then left the building.

The point: Fifteen minutes into his presentation, when the laser show wasn't wowing the audience, there was no substance to the conversation. In fact, I was beginning to question if he had any knowledge of the field.

... but back to the book ...

Your clients, my friend, have spent 15 minutes with everyone in town. They know the buzz words. They could practically write the book on BS related to what you and your peers want to sell.

Take a quick walk with me down memory lane. Arm in arm, let's stroll down our own little yellow brick history lesson and land ourselves in 1920. Maybe you're imagining a flock of flappers and prohibition-defying speakeasies, but I want to focus your distracted-self on a startling statistic.

According to the Bureau of Labor Statistics, in 1920, only 5% of the American population held professional jobs – and that included everything from actors to priests (and, oddly, included all workers 10 years old or greater ... ahh ... the good old days).

Add to that, the 1920s also saw that 40% of jobs were manufacturing and 25% were agriculture. A sum total of 65% of the population held jobs that we would only expect to watch Mike Rowe perform on the Discovery Channel.

Fast forward us into a hippie-frocked world, and 1965 saw the high point of manufacturing (reaching 65% of the total US economy). Then, like Bambi on skis, it started to take a nosedive, being replaced, of course, with a service-based economy. We, as a people, used to build things. Then we decided that other countries could do it cheaper and better, so we started selling our personalities.

We had been out-crafted, so we, the people, built a new economy which was supported by service-based professionals. We bleached those blue collars and started to sit at desks at disproportionate rates.

Seemed like an improvement, right?

Well, enter technology.

You, buddy, are now living in a world of virtual assistants and artificial intelligence. Your "customer service" number rings to New Delhi and your "friendly neighborhood stockbroker" has been replaced by Robin Hood himself.

Doomsday? Nah. We're too smart for that. We're American, after all. [insert patriotic 'Merica fist pump]

Where am I going with this, you ask? (Well, I'm glad you're still with me after all those numbers.)

Here is the scoop: Our economy over the last hundred years has changed so drastically that nearly everything has become commoditized. You, my friend, are replaceable.

Just like Tinder has introduced you to every available bachelor and/or bachelorette in a 25-mile radius, the global economy has now made you compete with Shanghai for a job.

Don't believe me? Well, that's too bad, because it's that attitude that keeps *you* stuck exactly where you are.

Let's just assume I know a thing or two and continue the conversation (well, I get to be more of a monologue at this point, so, with bated breath, hinge your future on this one thought).

Your mind is your only real asset in today's world.

Your personality and craftsmanship are great, but some raw bandwidth is more attractive to an employer / client / consultant than anything else you possess.

Clients are buying your mind. They've heard all the sales pitches before. They know you can build a website. They know you can take a pretty picture. They know you can smile when you answer the phone.

To that end, what makes you different? Why you?

Too many people enter conversations thinking about the "why not me" factor. Sure, the girl can pick you over everyone else, but that sounds like a lottery ticket more than a strategy. And 45 able-bodied people just applied for the job you wanted in the last 12 minutes.

Why you?

Why me?

Why Nancy Kerrigan? Why? Why now!?

(Sorry. I got distracted by the 1994 Winter Olympics. It happens.)

I'm back.

The answer to the "why" is found in your individuality. Quit focusing on what you need to do to "keep up" and start focusing on the things which make you an individual. Your uniqueness is what is going to sell you today – specifically, your *noggin*. That brain bank of yours is filled with thoughts that nobody else has ever thought (likely a good thing if your mind is anything like mine). You're hired for what you know, not what you don't know.

Folks come into my company every day, it seems, to start their first day at the new job. The ones that I can predictably say will fail are those who come in looking for the owners' manual for their position. Now, certainly training is important, but training should only be to train you for process. Training for cognitive ability or creativity is on you. I mean 100% on you.

The valuable person in the workplace isn't the guy who inputs all his numbers correctly and three hours earlier than everyone else. I already pay you to put everything in correctly and timely. You just proved you're average. Well done.

I remember having a conversation with a person at my office recently in which she defended some work by juxtaposing her experience to a peer. (First of all, bad plan for advancement, if your basis for value is comparison, but I'll ignore that.)

I took the opportunity to spend a few minutes explaining that the value found in her peer was (and is) not the answers that he possessed. His value is found in his ability to ask the right questions. His mind is curious. He looks for patterns and anomalies and tests them for duplicability. He finds ways to improve a process, rather than following one already in place. He predicts clients' questions in advance, because he's asking himself the same questions.

Not just a hat rack, folks. That 10-pound melon on your shoulders can set you apart from the pack.

Quick step back to our 'dinner and a movie."

Does any woman describe her husband as the ideal companion because he buys her roses on Valentine's Day? Or always comes home after work? Or has never had an affair?

Seems like some low standards, eh? He followed the rules though, right? The marriage process worked. Maybe he always saves 10% of his income. *That's so hot, right?*

What is she looking for? Those things, naturally, but that's what everyone does (or should). Don't put "telephone skills" and "Internet navigation" on your damn resume. No kidding!

She is looking for a guy who sends flowers to her office for no reason at all. Who surprises her with cards on the kitchen counter. Who plans a long weekend away without her knowledge.

She wants a guy who is above average. A guy who *thinks* about ways to excel and love well. It really isn't much to ask, ladies, so quit settling. Average guys and gals exist all over. Dare to set yourself apart – and demand that he/she does too.

When your fifteen minutes are over, what else are you adding to the conversation?

Squirrel! (If you're seen the movie Up, you'll understand.)

I remember years ago, seems like a lifetime, I was attending a board meeting for a company for which I worked. Prior to the board meeting, however, I had created a bingo board titled "Bullshit Bingo," and in each of the squares, I wrote a catch phrase or cliché which would be frequently used in these seemingly pointless meetings.

The CFO, who was a friend of mine, was a hilarious guy with a booming voice and hysterical sense of humor. So, naturally, I got a hold of his stack of financials and placed a copy of the bingo board on the top page. As the meeting began, he opened his folder and found this strategic distraction.

Besides the fact that he had tears rolling down his face throughout most of the meeting, embarrassing himself to the high heavens, it was the perfect demonstration of how ridiculous our meetings had become. With predictability, we were *silently* calling bingo within minutes (attempting to not make eye contact, of course, as the laughter would have become too evident).

You'll laugh, but as I am writing this chapter, I am making bingo boards to give to my clients. In each of the squares is going to be a box with an industry "buzz word" that our competitors are likely to use during their "pitches." I'm sure my clients will find it entertaining, but it makes the point that everyone is using the same language and the same hooks to close a deal.

Meanwhile, I'm just here trying to build relationships. I'm not closing deals; I'm making friends and expanding my network. If they want to do business with me, I'm flattered, but my primary objective is to add value to their lives.

Isn't that what a first date should look like?

If you don't add value to my already *amazing* life, pass.

And if I don't add value to your already *amazing-except-that-i-am-not-in-it* life, then pass.

What I will say, however, is that all the buzz words and pitches last only about 15 minutes. Maybe we're tied ... until minute 16. That's when I'm going to shine.

Personal Confession

Okay, so we're dipping back into the history books on this one. In fact, so far back that I may be in high school still for this story. Truth. Ugly, nerdy, insecure, awkward high school me. And, before you get all funny with the "what's changed?" punchlines, I'll beat you to the punch: not much. Well, one thing.

Confidence.

Not arrogance, mind you. Confidence. There's a difference.

So, high school. Dating a girl and I was convinced that she was clearly out of my league. And, my best friend, of course, was the guy that every girl wanted to date. Figures, right? Nothing builds confidence like spending all your time with people who are far above you. Geez! Great plan, right?

Then, one day, while hanging with my buddy, he says, "Hey, have you ever heard of this song by Jeff Healey?" The song was *Angel Eyes* (go download if you haven't). He continued, "It reminded me of you and your girl."

I'd love to say that it was a compliment, but I'm afraid I'm not sure it was. He meant well as he pointed out that the lyrics of the song played out like my life.

> *Now I'm the guy who never learned to dance.*
> *Never even got one second glance.*
> *Across the crowded room was close enough.*
> *I could look, but I could never touch.*

Yeah, my best friend.

Okay, it was true.

I can't even deny it.

But pay attention, because the best part is yet to come.

> *All you fellows, you can look all you like,*
> *But this girl, you see, she's leaving here with me tonight.*

There it is. It started out sounding like a bit of an insult, but at the end of song, there was a bit of a plot twist. Jeff Healey is asking himself questions throughout the lyrics, like "how did I ever win your love? What did I do? What did I say?" While he seemingly questioned the reasoning for their connection, he capstones the questions with confidence. Despite all his doubts, he accepts that she wants *him*. No further questions.

Now, some 25+ years later, I still think about that song. I still listen to those lyrics from time to time – but I have quit questioning why.

Not "why me?" But what value can I bring to this situation that will make me leave the winner? Confidently. What can I bring to the equation that others cannot? Then own it.

New client calls. My favorite.

Here we are in south Florida. Not the "305" (Miami), but the "954" (Fort Lauderdale). And we're on a client call with a potential client who is locally based. Typically, this makes me happy, because I'm a fan of knees-to-knees conversation, but this client didn't want to meet in person. They wanted to phone conference, because they didn't want to give a competitive advantage to any of the agencies they were interviewing (and most were out of state).

Fair. And well thought out, I will add.

Well, my call had been handled by the director of marketing and the COO. Our team did our virtual dog and pony show, as expected, but, if you know anything about me at this point, you'll know that I can't stand just "presenting a pitch." Remember, it isn't about the transaction; it is about the relationship.

Of course, while I do the pitch, I'm trying to find that common ground. I'm trying to learn something about them and how we can connect relationally. Then it happened.

I won't go into the details, but we found some common ground outside of the business pitch. We laughed a little and made small talk on the topic. My new business developer was looking at me like I had lost my mind. (Okay, maybe I have lost my mind, because the topic was politics. And who talks about politics with a potential client, right?)

The call continued and suddenly the conversation got even more comfortable. Now, I was talking to a person who trusted me. I was no longer a pitch guy. So, we just talked. Like friends.

As the call was winding up, I heard a new voice chime in.

"You're not typical 954," he said.

I hesitated, partly because I wasn't sure what that meant, but partly because this was a voice I hadn't heard before. "Oh, Mark, sorry. I didn't mention that our CEO joined the call a little bit ago. That was him speaking."

Me? I was just being me. I wasn't trying to impress the CEO. I didn't even know he was on the call. I was just doing what I do.

What did his remark mean? Well, his remark was just that I wasn't like any one of the local agencies that he had interviewed. As it turns out, they were not interviewing agencies from around the country. They wanted a local agency, but they didn't want to tell anyone that at first.

I stood out. I wasn't even trying to stand out. I followed my instinct and just did what I do. And, accidentally was recognized as "not being the typical 954."

Stick to your plan. Provide the value. Be of substance. Don't entertain and impress. Be.

Ryze-ing to the Occasion

If I'm being honest, but not conceited, I will tell you that I can make a good first impression. I understand the art of being charming and making small talk. It isn't that complicated, even if you're in a room full of people unlike yourself. It's acting.

But, the trickier part (for me anyway), is making a good second impression. And, to be even more honest, it is trusting that my team will live up to the first impression I made. After all, if I'm the first impression (assuming I made a good one), now everyone else needs to be just as impressive. You've likely surmised that I already have a plan for this, right? You're a smart one.

As the agency principal, it isn't a surprise that I am knowledgeable on most things that we do. That just makes sense, right? So, to the extent that I can likely talk about most subjects related to our business, it is equally as difficult to *not* talk about them.

My second impression strategy is to let my people be the experts.

If we have ever met, you know that I can talk for days (15 minutes is nothing). I'd like to believe I can also provide value past those 15 minutes too. I have learned, however, that if I am the only person on our team doing the talking, the client begins to devalue everyone else on my team. So, I have been forced to learn the art of "STFU."

It's a "good cop / bad cop" scenario. If I'm the charm, then I allow someone(s) else to provide the technical components. If someone else was the charm, then I can provide the expertise. I love to include my people in the conversation with clients, as it shows depth and skill, but I have also learned one other trick in this trade.

Allowing my people the ability to interact directly with my clients has given me the freedom to be the client's advocate (relationship). If I'm the guy doing the selling, and the client disagrees with something, I can't challenge my own pitch. I must either surrender or defend.

When my team presents and provides the technical explanations, and the client disagrees with something, I can advocate for the client and massage the conversation. I become the ringmaster, rather than the attraction. And it's a beautiful thing.

Today's Lessons Learned

- Charm lasts for about 15 minutes. After that, you better know what you're talking about.
- Clients are buying your mind. Your skills and personality can be outsourced in today's world.
- Meeting minimum expectations is not ever enough. Never settle for being mediocre.
- Your mind is your only real asset in today's world.

Now, Ask Yourself

- Self, when you're attempting to impress someone, are you relying too heavily on your charm and personality, or are you providing substance?
- Self, in what ways do you intentionally go above and beyond to set yourself apart from others with whom you are in competition?
- Self, what do you do to make yourself more socially relatable, when trying to find common ground? Be like your audience, in some way.
- Self, in what areas do you provide substance and value?

On "feeling it."

Chapter 5 ½: Chemistry Lesson
(Yes, I just did that. My book, my rules.)

Okay, now while I do understand that most of you are reading this book starting with the pages with the smallest numbers in the corners and working your way to the right, I wish that were the way that books were actually written. Oh, sweet Buddha's belly, if you knew the amount of back and forth goes into making sure that I have positioned you for the fan-STATIC world waiting for you at the end of this novella.

Why do I tell you about the asynchronous nature of the writing? Well, because this chapter slipped through the cracks very early in the draft and got added later. And, as anyone does while watching a movie reboot with "never before scenes," you spend an hour and a half trying to figure out which scenes were added. I'm just helping you out by identifying it here. THIS CHAPTER WAS ADDED LATER, but I *cannot, will not, could not, would not* allow this book to be published without this chapter being included.

So, getting back to our regularly-scheduled program, it's time for a little chemistry lesson.

Lesson: Nothing happens without chemistry.

Nothing. Happens. Without. Chemistry.

Nothing.

Happens.

Without.

Chemistry.

I think I have sufficiently made my point, but if not, imagine that I retitled this chapter, "The First Kiss." There you go. You get it.

First date is over. You're getting anxious thinking about how the night is going to end. Maybe you took some serious notes from chapter three and "prepared correctly, just in case." So be it.

(I'll give you a minute to flip back to chapter three to see what I'm talking about. HINT: Chapter three, bullet #3 under "Men.")

There we go.

Well, in any event, every date must end *somewhere*, right? Could be a gentle good night kiss. Could be a little more. Could be a high five and a fist bump. Who am I to judge?

But I do know one thing for certain: If something doesn't happen at that moment, there will be a lot of other really awkward moments in the very near future. This is a two-step process we're going to unpack here.

- Point #1: *Something must happen.* The date needs to end, right? And whether you each opt for the kiss, the high five, or a little *somethin' somethin'*, the consequences are permanent. The impression is made. The stage is set. Everything that just took place during the entire dinner date now rests on this one moment. Because, if this moment goes wrong, it doesn't matter how good dinner was – dessert sucked.

- Point #2: *Did dessert suck?* Once the decision is made, to kiss or not to kiss, a permanent memory is now forever imprinted on your psyche. Did the butterflies show up? Did it work for you both?

Assuming that we're focusing on a Disney audience here, we'll proceed with the understanding that we opted for a good night kiss – only.

Here you are, front door still locked but keys in hand, you flirtatiously make the "I'm not going to let this moment end" small talk (I swear I would give anything for a transcript – that sh#t is gold). You lean in. She doesn't quite do the same. You back off. She backs off. Now you're wondering why she backed off when you backed off. Maybe she was leaning in, and you missed the cue. Is it weird to ask? Oh, gosh! Did you misread a signal?

Seriously, it is like junior high school, completely relived in a 56-second flashback.

If she was not "signaling," you risk being too forward and ruining anything that *could* ever happen.

If she *was* "signaling," but you read it wrong, you just rejected her advance and you missed it.

Again, opportunities lost and never regained. Dignity stands toe-to-toe with desire, and you're caught in the middle with no life vest.

Been there? Done that? Didn't know how to ask? Assumed things went so well that it was obvious?

Maybe you relate more to the board meeting or the sales presentation when you did *everything* right and assumed that they would ask for a contract right on the spot. You bought lunch. You spent weeks putting together the perfect presentation. You even researched everything about their company to impress them with your knowledge.

They smiled throughout the whole meeting. They nodded along. They laughed at your jokes at all the appropriate times. Then, right at the end, you're left with the choice of having to be forward enough to *ask for the sale*.

It happens, but it is always a blow to the ego of anyone who feels confident that you have earned the signature. Then ... wham!

What went wrong? Why did it stop *flowing*?

The possibilities are endless, but as anyone who has ever received a side-hug at the end of a first date can attest, it really messes with your mind.

Want to know what was missing? I'll answer that for you.

Passion.

When the chemistry is right, nothing can stop it.

When the chemistry is wrong, nothing can make it happen.

It's just science.

PART II: The Chase

On having character.

CHAPTER 6: CHIVALRY IS NOT DEAD
(although it does seem to be limping a lot)

Confession: I was raised by my paternal grandmother, and I'm not ashamed to tell you that I was a "mama's boy." She loved me like crazy (more than all the other kids, honestly, but who can blame her?). Being the favorite is kind of fun. I never minded it. But, I'm going to tell you that there is one thing that nobody thinks about when it comes to being the favorite: the expectations.

Ah, the reverse side of that coin. Along with the attention and affection comes a lengthy list of expectations that were never imposed on the others. It's a lot of straight A, best behavior kind of … well, behavior. And, while being the golden boy certainly has its perks, it sometimes just plain sucks. My cousins could have practically shot up a bus full of nuns and there wouldn't be so much as a discussion on the topic.

Me? Well, I'll spare you the details, but anytime someone uses the word "disappointed" in a sentence, I tend to roll up in a ball like a hedgehog and rock myself to sleep.

Overall, it was good times though. I was a good kid, so there wasn't a lot of trouble, but, as an adult, I have found that those expectations have led me to be a door-holding, stand-on-the-subway, pay-the-tab, ladies-first, please-and-thank-you, yes-sir and yes-ma'am kind of guy.

It's all very Karate Kid, really. The lessons don't make sense until the teacher isn't in the room. Then, one day, you suddenly realize that you were being trained all along.

Those lessons, friends, have helped craft me into the man I am today. My grandmother's neurotic penchant for proper grammar had an impact. Her expectations that a man should treat a lady like a lady paid off.

The part that I find most surprising is that most women have stopped expecting that kind of treatment. They're so accustomed to lackluster, milquetoast excuses for men that they have stopped *demanding* it, in fact.

(If you are in any way offended by talk of gender roles, I encourage you to skip over the next section, as your opinion of me may fade. If you're already not enjoying this book though, please read on anyway, but please don't put a review on Amazon.)

MEN: Listen to me, hombres. I don't care what they tell you, there is no woman who wants to be treated like a dude. And, while I know I am going to take crap for saying this, it's my book and I get to write things down. Own it. You want a woman who "treats you like a man," first treat her like a lady. Court her. Romance her. It's more than flowers though, fellas. I'm talking about the kind of stuff that makes her remember why she chose you. It's courtesy. It's thoughtfulness. It's giving her space to be a woman and not being threatened by her. It's security. It's decisiveness. It's the grow-the-f-up-and-quit-acting-like-a-damn-boy kind of stuff.

WOMEN: Be women. Please. Quit accepting these men who won't even take the time to put your needs first. You're confusing the rest of us. We all have bad days, but there is nothing more harmful to a man's ego than having a woman be disrespectful toward him. Men crave the admiration of a woman, and when that is stripped away, expect things to go south. Being a strong independent woman is great, but I dare you to find ways to make him *want* to be the kind of man that you quit believing exists anymore.

Chivalry is not dead, friends. Severely wounded, I'll give you, but not dead.

And, since we're always drawing parallels to the world of business, what in the name of Mother Mary has happened to customer service!? Have people seriously just quit trying to meet a customer's needs?! Why are we surprised when someone provides good service?!

Like the Karate Kid, I have led you down this path, Daniel Son, talking all serious about relationships and such, but secretly making you question your expectations of people - the expectations that we place on each other. In business. In personal relationships. In families. In friendships.

Speaking to a couple of colleagues recently (oh, hell, let's be honest, I was mediating the dumbest fight you've likely ever heard), I kept repeating the phrase: "Nobody is mad about what anyone did. You're all just mad that nobody did what you expected."

Expectations can kill a person's spirit. It forces people to be compared to an unknown benchmark of performance. It's like shadowboxing. There is no winner, but you leave the room exhausted.

My best advice: Treat the other party as if you expect nothing in return. "He who *expecteth* not is never disappointed," they say.

So, here we are. Mr. Miyagi would be proud that we've now made three references to Ralph Macchio's epic performances. What in the name of Sam Hill does this have to do with dating? Or business? Or entrepreneurship in general?

I'll tell you.

Back to that dinner table with Ms. Right-Now. Your match.com romance has expectations of you that you'll never know about. She's silently judging everything you do and say. You're going through some bootcamp in her mind and you'll never know whether you're failing until you've already failed. Everyone is a winner, right up until they're not.

She's observing your manners. She's watching how you treat the waitress. She's trying to pick up on subtle cues of how you feel about family. It's a mine field, really, and until you have successfully passed the test, it doesn't matter how friendly, how handsome, how well-manicured, how wealthy, or how charming you are. The first test is getting through the gauntlet. One misstep and the game could be over.

Now, granted, we all do it. Men, just like women, make similar observations, although I would argue that the list is slightly different (sexist as that may seem).

And here is the kick in the pants: We do the same thing at work.

Imagine that you're courting a client for a big project that could be coming down the pass. Before any signatures are in ink, you better believe that folks are making observations of each other. They want to envision what this relationship will look like *after* the paperwork is signed. They're looking for any chink in your armor to reveal whether your attentive, Dunkin' Donut's delivery boy act is going to stick around past the contract signing.

Your clients watch for timeliness. They watch for frequency of contact. They watch for consistency. They watch to see if you reply to their messages in appropriate ways, or if you're always passing the buck to another colleague.

They want to know who we are as people. They want to know that you're in it past the deal. Your clients are looking for a partner – not a vendor. There is no reason for them to accept anything less because you're not the only gig in town.

How do you plan that though?

The same way you plan everything else: with intention.

Your client expects courtship and manners. They expect you to be on time and meet your commitments.

And why shouldn't they?

Like the first date analogy, they are putting you through a battery of tests in their minds to first decide if you meet their standards as a *person*. Remember, the personal relationship is so much more important than the product or the price. People buy from people (you'll hear me say that a lot).

Personal Confession

I'm in the market for a new home right now and I cannot even tell you how frustrated I am that I can't get a realtor to even pay attention to me. They want the business and jump around to get you to sign the agreement, but when they are required to follow up and do the work, things get lazy, I'm afraid. Maybe it's a South Florida thing, but I have never had this problem when living in other parts of the country. It's so strange.

For the love of money, if you're a commissioned salesperson (like realtors are), why wouldn't you pay attention to a potential client? Real story. Perhaps I'm bad at picking realtors, but I expect to be nurtured. I expect communication. I expect *you* to work to make me happy.

I have been keeping a log of actual things I have been told by realtors over the last year or so (I've also bought rental property, so don't think it has taken me a year to buy a house).

- "If you see something you like, just let me know." (Then why am I paying you? I'll just call the seller's agent.)

- "Sorry I didn't return your calls, but I went out of the country for a few weeks and didn't have access to cell service." (Thank you, ace. That made my home search much easier.)

- "It's normal for the buyer to pay the closing costs when you're buying from a bank." (First of all, this was told to me at closing. Secondly, it is not normal. And, for the love of all things holy, why wouldn't you have mentioned that before now!?)

- "I've been wanting to get into doing more volunteer work, and I know you do a lot. Can I join you next time?" (Of course, but then you never returned my calls or showed up for the volunteer work. She tried to engage personally, but then failed miserably at follow up.)

- "After I looked at the house you requested to see, I don't think you'll like it, so I took it off the list." (Huh?)

All of these are real stories, and I have so many more. And, while I'm probably really bad at picking realtors, I can't believe that folks actually do these things when they work on commission only.

Still stunned.

From the CEO's Desk

Admittedly, my expectations for customer service are right off the charts, but the reason is simply because an extra 10% of effort can earn you 100% of my business. It is just math. And, while I'm willing to admit that, as a business owner, my standards are likely higher (because I see the economics differently), it literally makes my brain melt when I see people do stupid things that cost the company countless dollars in business. (Also, a pet peeve is when people use the word "literally," rather than "figuratively" or "metaphorically.")

At our sister company, *eConcierge* (www.eConcierge.solutions is another of my companies which does outsourced customer service and sales support), we have a client who *literally* decided to remove their phone number from their website – because they didn't want people calling to complain.

[moment of silence in memory of common sense]

True story. We used to handle their telephone support and sales, and at the disposition of each of those calls, we would have either handled the customer's complaint, or escalated it to someone at their office for follow-up. In response to the number of complaints they were receiving about their products, they decided that they were going to remove the phone number from the website so that people couldn't complain.

You can't make this stuff up.

If we're going to translate this to relationships, it is the equivalent of a man putting in earplugs so that he and his wife would quit fighting. It will make for a happier marriage, after all.

That, apparently, is how you do customer service.

(NOTE: This is a large, online, national brand. This is not a small company with a shady story.)

RYZE-ING TO THE OCCASION

There are a few phrases which are not allowed at our office. Some of the obvious ones are things like "that's not my job" and "nobody told me to." I mean, nothing says "teamwork" like blame. [dramatic eye roll]

But, if I may be honest, there is one phrase that will never be accepted here – yet it still slips into conversations. And, it is still met with sarcastic, exasperated glares.

The phrase: "*I sent an email and am just waiting for a reply.*"

The standard response: "*Did you call?*"

You see, I find email to be offensive. I mean, I use it all day long, but it is a poor excuse for service. It is transactional. The "I sent an email" is the equivalent of "I'm not to blame for the failure anymore, because I threw the ball into someone else's court."

It's cheap. It's quick. It's non-committal. And I hate it when my people use it as an inhumane form of communication.

Like it or not, email can be dehumanizing. If I cannot have knees-to-knees, in-person communication, I'll accept a Zoom call. If I can't get a Zoom call, I'll accept a phone call. If I can't get a phone call, I'll accept an email. But only as a last resort.

Do not, and I repeat, DO NOT, sacrifice your relationships on the altars of transactions.

Today's Lessons Learned

- In the world of customer service, you are not competing against your own standard, but the customers' expectations.
- Treat the other party as if you expect nothing in return.
- They want to know who we are as people. They want to know that you're in it past the deal. Your clients are looking for a partner – not a vendor.
- Clients are more interested in character than courtship.

Now, Ask Yourself

- Self, in what ways do you express the importance of relationship to the people in your life?
- Self, are you the same person after the "big transaction"?
- Self, have you ever been held accountable to someone else's expectations? Did you find yourself becoming a better person because of it? (Sometimes, other people make us 'level up.')
- Self, what expectations do you have of people? How do you explain that to them, rather than just making them guess?

On avoiding shortcuts.

Chapter 7: Pheromone-Infused Perfumes Are En Vogue

The date is 1994. *Z Cavaricci* is still dominating the world of fashion, and the Ford Probe still looks like a wedge of cheese. It was a simpler time.

And for those of you who were in high school, or even college, at that time, you will recall the introduction of the magical, pheromone-infused cologne, *Realm* (although there were a lot of them back then).

True Statement: I owned a bottle.

The brand's claim was that it was infused with actual human pheromones, which makes the wearer irresistible to the opposite sex. They claimed that the cologne was infused with the animalistic, carnal scent that makes a woman go randy for a man (or vice versa). This infusion of pheromones was hailed to produce an insuppressible sexual response.

(For those readers who are interested, some quick research found that you can still buy Realm at your local CVS store. But, given the likely success of this book, you'll have to act quickly before the rest of the free world gets to chapter 7.)

(And, if you happen to be an executive at Realm, *please sign me up for your affiliate program. I expect my 5% cut on all these CVS sales.)*

For the scientifically minded among us, these magical elixirs work a little something like this (theoretically, of course):

- Clear liquid secretions in a man's genital, under arm, and navel regions contain pheromones.
- This musky scent is infused into the cologne and is subconsciously detected by a woman's olfactory system (the nose knows).
- The olfactory system then bypasses the rational brain.
- The smell triggers a woman's natural response (attraction) to a healthy, fit, fertile man, without her brain first knowing.
- She would respond like a cavewoman and immediately want him to father her children.

What I just read: Ball sweat from any random guy, when added to cologne, makes women lose all inhibitions.

...

...

...

...

[please excuse the author momentarily as he is hurling uncontrollably in the restroom]

...

...

...

...

Okay, I'm back now.

Sounds fairly scientific, eh? Have a man spray some other man's juices on himself and women will go wild. (*Realm* was also not a fan of hygiene, I suppose.)

Call me old fashioned, but this just doesn't seem like a very good strategy for landing the perfect mate. One quick spray and women will be throwing themselves at you. Seems like a stretch, if you ask me, yet, they were able to make a load of money.

Why?

Because they weren't selling cologne. They sold a *shortcut* – an *outcome*. They sold an alternative to having to attract a woman the good old-fashioned way. I could skip the grooming and the courtship. So long as I had a spray of *Realm*, there was nothing that could make this night end badly.

Now, in fairness, and I don't care who you are, we would all love that to be true. The dream of a love potion didn't start with *Realm*, but they were able to capitalize on our naivete. We're that desperate for shortcuts that we'll try anything.

Lose 30 pounds in 12 days.

Mail in diplomas from fake universities.

Love at first sight.

Free trip to the moon.

Win a million dollars by only investing one dollar in a lottery ticket.

It's the guaranteed success that we all hope for – without the good ol' work-for-it sweat equity that it takes to plant your flag proudly and declare victory.

Shortcuts are attractive. They promise short-term pain for long-term gain. They intrigue us to believe that we have a chance (distant as the sun, of course, but a chance) to tip the scales of balance in our own favor and gain an unfair advantage. And who do you think would be first in line for those odds?

Well, I can answer that: *folks who didn't stand a chance in the first place.*

THE FUGLY TAX

Wander with me down to the 7-Eleven and let's dream about all our wishes coming true, will you? I mean, it only costs a dollar, if you pick the right numbers. And, with that kinda math, who wouldn't want to join?

(You wanted to join me, didn't you? Sad.)

Well, you may or may not be surprised to know this, but a lot of research has been done on the psychology of the lottery system. In fact, much of it has been done to understand the reasons why poor people overwhelmingly outspend ... well, *not-poor* people ... when it comes to the purchasing of lottery tickets. I mean, if you don't have any money to start, why spend what you *do* have on a 1 in 51,000,000 chance?

This phenomenon has led to the lottery's nickname: "the poor tax."

Get this: According to Bankrate's study in 2019, the lowest income bracket (those earning less than $30,000 / year) spent an average of 13% of their annual income on lottery tickets. A similar study published by the *Journal of Risk and Uncertainty* (for the record, who the hell works at this place?) reported that their estimate is that poor people (defined as those making less than $13,000 / year) spend an average of 9% of their annual income on lottery tickets (roughly $1,100 / year).

(STFU! If you are not at least *half* as shocked as I was in reading those statistics, well … let me sell you some *Realm.*)

Seriously though, those are staggering numbers. But I suppose they make sense when you correlate those studies to the work conducted by Kahneman and Tversky (1979) on *prospect theory*. Kahneman and Tversky examined how investors value gains and losses differently, placing more weight on perceived gains versus perceived losses. I won't bore you with the details but will say that it is fascinating stuff.

The research examined how the behavior exhibited by investors is the same as that observed in the purchasers of lottery tickets. Net in effect, individuals tend to choose options which are framed as a potential gain, rather than options framed as a potential loss.

That is, winning the lottery is a far greater motivator than the fear of *losing* the cost of the ticket. To further this theory, several studies report that poor people tend to purchase lottery tickets at higher rates simply because the net effect would be greater to their lives. Going from *poor* to rich is a more attractive life change than going from *comfortable* to rich. They are more eager for a change. Maybe even desperate, you might say.

And, like the lottery, our friends at *Realm* managed to promise their consumers a party-hopping, heart-stopping, panty-dropping experience – all for the low, low price of a few squirts of cologne.

Which brings me to the "fugly tax."

Just like the lottery is considered a tax on the poor (i.e., because of their desperation for a long-shot success), I propose that *Realm* took advantage of me at the tender age of 19. There I was, a total long-shot candidate for "Friday night success," but *Realm* made me believe that I had a chance – distant as it may have been.

(I started this chapter asking for an affiliate commission on sales, but now I think I'm going to start researching class action lawsuits. Stay tuned.)

Tip from a Pro: *Don't count on shortcuts.* Seldom do they pan out, but they also distract you from putting in the real work it takes to accomplish a goal.

On Instant Gratification

The world is filled with get-rich-quick scams and schemes. Over the years, I've watched hundreds of them rise to popularity, then vanish as quickly as they began. It's not surprising, after all, as they seldom offer real promise. It's just an illusion which appeals to a culture riddled with the demand for instant gratification.

Do you look for this professionally? Do you look for the clients who are willing to sign anything, even though you know it is not going to end well? Do you look for the too-good-to-be-true investment opportunities?

They're real questions. You, like me, are attracted to fast success. But it rarely ends up that way.

The most recent phenomenon, of course, is this world of social media and influencer marketing. Everyone with a smart phone is persuaded to believe that she can become an instant success. "After all," she'll argue, "if _____ can do it, why can't I?"

Fair question, I guess, but we are only ever looking at the two-dimensional world of Instagram. We know nothing of the behind-the-scenes work. We know nothing of her contacts. We know nothing of how many years it took to get there. Yet, here you are, princess, trying to selfie your way to success.

Business owners, stop trying to land the "big fish," and realize that the most successful businesses grow over time through commitment and perseverance. Any snake oil salesman can sell a variety of elixirs which promise instant love / success / odor reduction, but if your commitment is to real results, nothing beats hard work.

Shortcuts, friends, provide nothing but myopic results. Effort, I propose, is directly correlated to output.

Think about that.

Now apply it to your budget.

Now your workouts.

Now your business.

Follow?

Can we agree that *personal* relationships take work too? In fact, more work than you would ever expect – especially during the butterfly stages of courtship - but all good things are worth the investment. The same way that you commit to your business, you must apply that kind of effort and commitment to winning at your marriage (or love life, if things haven't gotten that serious yet).

I'm going to let you write your own section on relationships this time but will leave you with these questions for provocation. In your personal life:

- When thinking about your partner, are you treating the relationship like an "ongoing concern" or just "hoping it works out"?

- Are you expecting long-term results, but only giving short-term effort?

- Does your partner understand your level of commitment to your relationship?

- In what ways are you putting in lasting effort?

- How would someone on the outside know that you are investing in your future together?

Now go do your homework.

Personal Confession

One of my favorite authors is Malcolm Gladwell. I dare say that we do not share a sense of humor, but the man is clearly remarkable in his ability to "thin slice" (his words, not mine) human behavioral phenomenon. One of my favorite books he has written: *Tipping Point*.

In this book, Gladwell purports that it takes a minimum of 10,000 hours to gain efficacy at *any* skill – whether that be playing basketball to playing the violin, or graphic design, or cooking, or authoring a book. Net in effect, he believes that it takes five years to get good at something, if you make it a full-time commitment.

Upon my first reading of this fact, I became acutely aware of the times I quit too soon. Frustrated that I wasn't a naturally-gifted prodigy, I gave up before I likely even hit my first 1,000 hours. If I wasn't an expert in the first week … month … year … it must not have been for me.

I then started thinking of all the people that I know whose "gifts" and "talents" are so well crafted that they seem to make it look effortless.

I thought about friends who have perfect physiques (and then realized the hours they spent at the gym).

I thought about friends with musical talents which are remarkable (and then realized the hours they spent practicing their instrument).

I thought about friends with businesses which flourish, seemingly without their active involvement (and then realized the hours they spent building that empire).

I then realized that I had likely spent more than 10,000 hours criticizing myself for not being "more talented" or "more gifted" than I am. And, as Gladwell would have predicted, I got good at it.

It was an awakening, for sure. Maybe some regret got baked in there, but it resulted in a lot of forgiveness. The good old fashioned "me forgiving me for not being perfect" kind of forgiveness. It was liberating.

Anything worth having is worth working for.

If you want the talent, work for it.

If you want the client, work for it.

If you want the girl, work for her.

From the CEO's Desk

I've mentioned, several times, stories about being approached with "lightning in a bottle" ideas. Products that couldn't fail. Companies which were *guaranteed* to succeed. Yet, I have learned two particularly important things over the course of my career:

1. I am an optimist, right down to the marrow.

2. Few things in this life come without some hard work.

Years back, I had a mentor who will never know the impact that he had on my life. I wish he were around to tell him, but this guy just had a way of seeing the world that always made me stop and listen. (Well, half the time I was trying to figure out whether he was being sarcastic.)

In his office one day, we happened onto a personal conversation, which seldom happened. He was an incredibly quiet guy, so "chit chat" wasn't his strength. I was sharing with him that someone had made some comments about my recent success. I had worked ridiculously hard and gave every ounce of my energy to that accomplishment, so I was likely quite defensive of the cattiness.

"You're a lucky guy," he said matter-of-factly, then turned to his computer and started typing an email or something.

(This is an example of a time when I would sit quietly to figure out if he was being sarcastic.)

Imagine the look on my face if my brain were trying to calculate the square root of 56,385,334. Same look, I'm sure.

He looked me square in the eye and shook his head. "You have a great car, a big income, a beautiful house on the beach. Just so lucky."

[crickets]

"And it seems like the harder you work, the luckier you just keep getting. It's as if there's a connection."

There it was.

If Taylor Swift were a 70-year-old white man from the hills of northern Georgia, I may have heard him say, "Haters gonna hate."

It was a positive affirmation, albeit strangely wrapped, but he took the time to acknowledge the amount of work that it took to get to where I was. He knew that there are no short cuts. He didn't compliment my success; he complimented my commitment to the journey – and that felt even better.

Today's Lessons Learned

- Don't count on shortcuts. Seldom do they pan out, but they also distract you from putting in the real work it takes to accomplish a goal.
- Treat the other party as if you expect nothing in return.
- The odds of winning the lottery are not in your favor. Don't spend 13% of your income on tickets.
- Never cover yourself in anyone else's sweat.

Now, Ask Yourself

- Self, in what ways do you invest hope in long-short, uncontrollable investments?
- Self, how are you investing in your daily relationships with the same type of investment you make in your professional life?
- Self, do you tend to *hope things will work out*, or do you hunker down and commit to the work to make it happen?
- Self, do you ever find yourself squandering resources, including your time, on things which have extremely low yield? Can you reinvest those resources towards more long-term gains?

On handling disappointment.

Chapter 8: Left On Read | The Cyber Stalker

(alternative title: "All of the Ghost; None of the Swayze")

So, ask yourself a quick question, but be sure to answer honestly, because we are about to do a little roleplaying here.

In every would-be relationship, someone is always into someone more than someone else is. Would you agree? Especially in those early days, week, months. And nobody wants to be the vulnerable one.

"Oh my gosh! He's so perfect! But if I tell him, I'll look too desperate."

"Dude, she's the one. I'll marry her. I just want to be sure that she's into me before I tell her. Too much and I'll scare her away."

So, you go on a date – or even a few dates – and, as best you can tell, things are going well. You've been getting all the signs: she's been affectionate in public; she's allowed you to touch the small of her back; she makes a point of indulging in all of the necessary courtship rituals which are expected in the western world (apologies to our non-western fans, but I have to write to my audience right now... they're paying the bills).

Perfume. Heels. A little extra eye liner. She's into you, right? Why else would she go to such lengths to get your attention. It would just be cruel to imagine that she would do all of this just to vanish. I mean, right? Do you think she'd do that? Be honest. No, of course she wouldn't. Right? *Right?*

The paranoia begins. But, not without cause.

On your way to paradise, the train somehow derailed. Like, a detour to the tenth power, and your head just can't take it. With stroke-like drool cascading down your perfectly manicured face (just the way she likes it), you stare at that phone. One word haunts your very existence: "Read." It's a subtext beneath that beautiful message you last sent, but now it taunts.

You begin questioning yourself as to whether you said too much. Was that last text too long? Too soon? Could she have taken it wrong? Perhaps you should text again and explain what you meant – just in case she read it wrong?

She's offended. You know it. You ruined this. You pushed it too far and now those three little dots control your world (for the prehistoric among us, the dots are the ones indicating that your contact is in the process of replying). Maybe you saw them, if only for a brief moment, but then nothing.

In the world of the "cyber hip" (the use of this phrase is an automatic disqualification for me, by the way), we call that "ghosting." As ethereal as the phantom presence of a dead relative repeatedly reliving a bad memory from the afterlife, she's gone. Like she never existed. As if you never knew each other. No goodbye. No reason given. Just a message left "on read."

(Firsthand experience be damned, we charge forward with our story.)

Perhaps you have been fortunate enough to never be on the receiving end of such an experience. Or perhaps you're frequently on the receiving end of this experience. Regardless (or should I say "irregardless," just to freak out the more literary of my readers), I think that everyone can empathize with what I'll call "the vanishing."

Someone, for some reason, didn't reply. Obsessively, we relive every moment of this short-lived relationship and wonder what went wrong.

Convincing yourself that you "just want to know why," you forge on, lying to yourself. Why do you want to know so badly? Because rejection hurts.

There it is. I said it.

Rejection hurts. It sucks. It is like watching the slow death of your self-worth, inching its way to utter devaluation. It's bad enough that you were not the "beau of choice," but the fact that you weren't even worth a courtesy call? Or even a text. Carrier pigeon. Smoke signal. That's too much for most rational people to wrap their heads around. It defies human decency, and regardless how much we swear that we don't care what *bishes* think, we do.

And, ladies, OMG! As a man, I can't even imagine what you go through with this hand-crafted recipe for internal disaster.

"The Vanishing" leaves a vacancy. It is limbo. It is the love child of mystery, disbelief, and hope, all blended with a "self-nurturing" chaser. The human brain wants to know what happened and why. And, this marks the only time in the life of a man or woman when the words "it's not you" would bring relief. At least there are words.

So, what do you do about it? Do you stay in bed hurling insults at your non-responsive smart phone? Do you commiserate with Ben and Jerry, knowing that you'll have to soon get your Richard Simmons on to counteract an evening of bad choices?

Often, and listen to this, we settle for texting the one person we know will reply.

[gasp with me]

Call it what you will (in some circles, it is called a "booty call"). I'm not implying that you're trying to *get ... it ... on*. I'm saying that your now-fragile psyche cannot stand the possibility that you are undesirable, so you reach out to someone who will put your delicate ego at ease.

We call it "settling" here in the western world (once again catering to my western-focused audience).

Here you are, on a Friday night, calling the person you swore you would never call again, romanticizing the moments that once carried you into a personal hell of regret. And all of this happens because we want to feel valued.

But I ramble. (I know you're shocked by this admission, but the first step in recovery is admitting you have a problem. Bear with me.)

And now for the much-anticipated transition into our parallel professional universe (visualize my well-selected PowerPoint animation).

[fade to black]

You've been working a client for months. Things look good. In fact, you have even been including this client on your quarterly sales projections. You've been meeting with contractors to install the new pool at your house in anticipation of your bonus check (a la Chevy Chase in Christmas Vacation).

Go ahead. Flash back to your favorite moment from that movie. Epic. (My favorite moment was the cat chewing on the Christmas tree lights.) #dogsrule

Anyway, so you're already fantasizing about how this client is already closed. In fact, you may give yourself a bit of a break from working your other leads because this one is coming through (think Tinder, eh?).

Then ... ghost.

The client quits returning phone calls. Doesn't answer emails. The contract is still sitting in your DocuSign account with status "read."

So, the client reviewed the contract. They agreed to it verbally. No flags on the play. We had lunch, dinner, drinks. All was well.

What do you do? You've already tallied this one as a win.

[scrolls back a few pages and copies some text]

"You begin questioning yourself as to whether you said too much. Was that last [message] too long? Too soon? Could [the message] have been taken wrong? Perhaps you should message again and explain what you meant – just in case?

"He / she is offended. You know it. You ruined this. You pushed it too far and now those three little dots control your world."

Parallel universes again.

So, what is it about the client's ghosting that sets us over the edge? What do we do about it? After all, as much as we hate to admit it, it's an emotional event. It becomes so much more than the commission check. It is more than the "big fish" story. This is personal. We connected. We shared meals and really "got" each other.

You're back at the drawing board trying to figure out what went wrong. Trying to figure out where you could have done better. How could this have been avoided? Is it me? Did I read something wrong? Am I just bad at [sales, closing, dating, reading situations, etc.]?

The roller coaster begins, but now what?

Like with that "perfect" date, life goes on without him/her. And it does so at a pace which doesn't allow you to sit around feeling sorry for yourself. There are bills to pay.

And, my friend, I'm here to tell you something: **It isn't you.**

Never.

Ever.

Ever.

I'll agree that you can be a bit of a tool every now and then. And you've likely offended some clients (and some dates) along the way, but poor communication will never be your fault.

Clients will be stupid. They'll marginalize your needs every time. We all talk about "partners" when we refer to clients and vendors, but let's get real. The primary responsibility of any employee or business owner is to nurture their own business first. They must make their own payroll before they care about yours. And they know that in a dog-eat-dog market, their business will still bring you back smiling and pretending like nothing is wrong.

I could spend days talking about the times I was forced to paste on a smile and pretend that a client's bad behavior didn't bother me.

I recently had a client walk my firm through an entire project: strategy, design, implementation, and the like. They hadn't paid a dime toward the project but argued the entire time. Then, suddenly, just stopped returning calls. Suddenly. We sat with all this work and didn't know what they were going to do. No responses at all. Project never mentioned again. We're sitting with a $200,000 project and don't even have a breakup letter.

Add insult to injury, the client reached out a month later regarding another project, like nothing had ever happened.

Would it have been easy to be bitter? Of course.

Would I have loved to have snubbed them the next time? Of course.

Pragmatism kicked in, however, and I knew that it wasn't anything to do with me. I did everything I was asked to do, and *they* behaved badly. So noted. And, at our next engagement, I assure you that the rules had changed. Our 50% down policy was never stronger. Our attention to documentation and performance-based billing was in full defense mode.

I could have simply cut bait with the client altogether, but there was still money to be made from them – just differently. And we did.

Tale as old as time (although I think I have used this cliché once before already, even asking you to sing along with me, if I'm not mistaken), we were bitten once and are twice shy.

Disappointment is part of relationships. And relationships always involve humans. And humans are, above else, self-preserving. And self-preservation almost always acts in the disinterest of the other party.

If all of this doesn't sound *Good Will Hunting* enough for you yet, let me repeat: "It's not your fault ... *it's not your fault.*"

You, princess, cannot own the bad behavior of others.

Dates will disappoint. They will leave you "on read" and vanish.

Clients will disappoint. They will leave you hanging for weeks or months, then come back like nothing happened.

And that's okay. What kills us is the letdown. The gap between expectation and reality hurts. We anticipate one thing and receive another.

If there is a lesson to be had from being left "on read," it is this: "Our expectations of others can neither change our value of ourselves, nor our value of others."

I often use the phrase "control the controllables." Only feel the need to act on the items which are within your ability to control them. There is no reason to assign guilt or blame to situations or behaviors which are outside of your purview. It's impractical and unproductive.

Personal Confession

I'm no stranger to the ghosting process. I suppose if I'm being honest, I've both been the ghost and been the ghosted. My greatest takeaway, having been seated on both sides of this table: The temporary discomfort of providing closure to the other party far outweighs the guilt of leaving him/her "on read."

I recall a relationship once that "experienced some turmoil." Things seemed to be going well – until they weren't. Every time there was even the slightest disagreement, she'd vanish. Literally, while on a vacation once, she booked a ticket home and left while I was in the hotel shower. (That situation got progressively more entertaining when her flight was canceled, and she got stuck at the airport for the night.)

Some time would pass, then I would hear from her, and we would reconnect. Then, like clockwork, it would happen again.

It took me quite some time to accept that this was not a situation I could fix. This pattern of behavior led to me *work harder.* I can fix anything, I foolishly believed. Almost like a puzzle that I was determined to solve. Call me a sadist, but even after three or four more of these abrupt endings, I kept going back. Repeatedly, I would accept responsibility for what was happening, because I just couldn't understand how someone could behave the way she did. (Ever ask yourself some really jacked up questions attempting to justify someone else's actions?)

By accepting the blame, I was granting myself the power to change things. If I were the problem then I could somehow change the input that kept leading to this output, right? Wrong. I would spend days, weeks, months trying to figure out what was going wrong, until I finally got smart enough to accept that it wasn't me. I was trying to control someone else's behavior – and I'm just not that powerful.

Also, I always make sure that hotel reservations are in my name, regardless with whom I am traveling. It's just safer that way.

From the CEO's Desk

Just today, this very principle played out in my professional life.

Months ago, we were introduced to a brand which is *painfully* in need of help. Painfully. Because it was a referral (and the referral let me know that they had money), I spent quite a bit of time with the owner. Call after call, I provided him with a lot of strategy and education about how he should position his brand, how to roll this product out to the public, and how he should position himself as the product spokesperson. It was all good advice, and he ate it up.

Fast forward, the time came when I finally had to ask the guy if he was going to use any of the services we provide (all of which he needed). His response was typical: "If you would, put it in a proposal for me and I'll review."

Now, you've taken hours of my time and been taking notes during every conversation, and now you want me to memorialize everything in a formal proposal, as if we had just met.

Fine. I'll play.

Ten pages later, I had crafted a proposal outlining all the things we had discussed over the prior weeks. Strategy. Execution. Creative. Everything.

Within less than 24 hours of sending it to him, I received this reply: "Thanks for this. We've decided not to use you guys."

You can imagine my reaction, but I held it together and followed my own advice.

Did I provide good advice? Yes.

Did I do everything I had agreed to do? Yes.

Did I do anything I regretted doing? No.

Then, it must have been him. Life goes on.

Well, fast forward to today. I received a pleasant surprise of an email from him. After having spent the last several months working on the project himself (and with others, I presume), he asked for a meeting to discuss hiring us.

Guess it wasn't me after all.

Ryze-ing to the Occasion

Around our place, we have a solid best practice: Do unto others as you would have them do unto you. I'm pretty sure that's good advice for life in general, or so I've heard, but we really try to keep integrity first in everything we do. We will always take the high road (and trust me, the views are much better from up here).

After having our contract terminated by a client some months back when a new marketing director was hired, I was amused at how the individual felt that she had to create an adversarial relationship with our team. We practically giftwrapped everything when the new company took over their marketing. Literally, everything we could do to help the migration was done at our own cost – and we did it anyway.

Fast forward several months, they're failing. And, while I take no pleasure in their struggle, when I learned that things were not going well, I slept easy that night knowing that it had nothing to do with us. We took the high road and moved on.

The interesting thing is that most people seem to want to be enemies when things are ending. We don't find that to be necessary and *never* treat people as if they're bad for not choosing us. If it isn't a match, save us the headache of trying to make it work too!

Today's Lessons Learned

- Other people's behaviors are not my responsibility.
- People cannot be held accountable to the expectations I place on them.
- My value is not - in any way - dependent on the value others place on me (both personally or professionally).
- When things don't go my way, it is my responsibility (not others') to cope with the disappointment and not internalize it as rejection.

Now, Ask Yourself

- Self, when was a time when you felt rejected and internalized it – irrationally? Did you later find out it had nothing to do with you?
- Self, when you are ignored (left on read), what is your typical reaction? Do you overreact or obsess? Do you overcommunicate?
- Self, have you ever spent time designing a method for proper follow-up? Has it been effective?
- Self, do you do this same thing to other people? Isn't karma a b#tch?

On learning trust.

Chapter 9: It's All About Trust

I'm starting from the end this time and working my way to the beginning. To start, a real-life example to illustrate the point I have yet to make (always keeping you guessing, eh?).

To recap, I operate an advertising agency which specializes in anything I decide to call our specialty (vis a vi the last conference call). I talk to clients, and potential clients, all day long - many of which are in no way prepared to work with us. Many I would not want to work with, as they are not a good cultural mix for us (and that matters so, so much).

Well, recently, a client forwarded an email to me from a marketing company which has reached out to him and offered him 'guaranteed results' (this is simply the most recent of many times this has occurred so I wasn't entirely surprised). His comment on the forward read: "You guys are the experts. Can you let me know your thoughts on this?"

My thoughts?

You forward me a solicitation email from another marketing company and ask me to "chime in"? What do you think I'm going to say? That's like your spouse asking if you think she would be more compatible with some other dude she recently met in a chat room.

If you're anything like me, or just prone to made-for-television over-dramatizations (or, perhaps that's redundant), you'd likely be thinking something along the lines of, "ARE YOU *SERIOUS* RIGHT NOW?! THIS IS WHERE WE ARE?!"

(Some Chandler Bing-like sarcasm may creep in at this point. "Could they *be* any more clueless?")

We're in a contractual relationship. Our firm is doing magnificent work for him - at discounted rates, I'll add, as we are trying to help him out because he's a nice guy (I'm a sucker for a sad story), and he forwards me an email from a random marketing company.

Random.

Did I mention this email was "random"?

My head nearly exploded.

Here we are fielding your Marketing 101 questions daily and coaching you, *pro bono*, on how to establish analytics to keep your sales team performing. We're rebuilding your website and generating lower cost leads than you've seen in your lifetime, and some other marketing agency was able to catch your eye with an email?

Trust? Loyalty? Reliability?

So, after a mantra of breathing exercises and a bit of an interoffice tantrum, I put it in check and went on with my day.

The facts, however, are ridiculous. The client is likely the smallest client in the building. We even offered them credit terms for their site rebuild because they didn't have the cash to pay for it (but were never going to convert a single sale on the site they had). And I also paid them $3,600 to allow three staff members to "sample" their services. The loss of this client wouldn't even alter a percentage point on our P/L, but it was offensive. It got me fired up, if you can't tell.

And a lesson was learned. Because lessons are always learned. Well, lessons are always *taught*; they are not necessarily *learned*.

1. The fact that he was so easily distracted by the "guaranteed results" email is not, and was not, a reflection on our performance. I impulsively questioned whether we were doing quality work for this company (or whether he just didn't see the value). I internalized.

2. The fact that he didn't see how his "wandering eyes" could hurt our relationship was not a reflection on us. It is data regarding his expectation of the relationship, and its non-exclusivity. By letting us know that he would be willing to entertain other marketing partners (out of what I can best describe as clumsy ignorance), he has potentially, and unwittingly, diminished the level of loyalty we will reciprocate to him.

3. Our team will not and cannot be impacted by a client's inability to navigate the waters of relationship. Clients, often ignorant of the implied messages they are sending, offend. Usually, they don't mean it, but they do it anyway. And our team is 100% committed to not internalizing a client's unintentional – or sometimes intentional – ill will.

4. Our team watches the behaviors displayed by our own clients and takes specific action to not *become* those clients to our vendors. We learn from the mistakes of others and vow to always value the relational over the transactional.

I want you to read that last sentence one more time:

Value the relational over the transactional.

Let that sink in for a minute.

Have you ever been in a situation when "being right" felt like you were losing something? It's that.

I'm a really good debater. I mean, I'm really, really good. Like, a master debater. And it has taken a lot of years to understand that winning isn't the goal of debate. The goal of debate is *understanding*.

Once again, let me give you a minute with that one.

The goal of a debate is not to win. It is to understand and be understood.

Are you hearing me, western world (sorry, I had to throw that in there for those of you who were offended by it in the last chapter)? Am I making sense? Can I get an amen?

True debate only takes place when both parties are attempting to understand the other – not win the joust. If I understand the other party's position, it does not mean that I must agree with it, by the way. It simply means that I can validate it, then provide probable reasoning for a difference of opinion.

Winning isn't the goal. I would rather have a person understand me and alter his/her opinion (thus earning a well-vetted ally) than stand over my victim's body in ceremonial victory. One earns me a trophy. The other a friend.

In the case of my client and his awkward inquiries, I want to discuss the relationship which was damaged.

If you were a member of my team and a client sent that inquiry, think about how you would have responded. It would likely be something like, "We're doing great work for this guy, and he doesn't appreciate it. I'll devote my attention to the clients that appreciate our work." Or, perhaps, "This guy is going to leave soon anyway, so why bother putting in any extra time on his account?"

I don't believe my client thought through any of these possible outcomes, but I can only say this from a position of relational maturity. I get what happened. I really do. But if that message were delivered to any other organization, they may have seen it as the client seeking an exit strategy.

Let me acknowledge that I understand that if he were really attempting an exit, he would be a fool to show his hand that way. His actions, nevertheless, hinted otherwise.

Transactionally, he did nothing wrong. He didn't threaten. He didn't accuse. He didn't say anything related to being unhappy with our work. In fact, he could argue that he trusted us so much that he was comfortable asking the question.

Relationally, however, he played the part of Brutus to our J.C. He didn't behave much like a partner, and my team was sensitive to that nuance. Amid juggling clients' priorities and deadlines, my team felt it was a sharp poke in the belly.

Et tu?

It's a torpedo to any relationship – this issue of trust. To be in a position of vulnerability and fear that the other party does not have your best interest in mind makes the heart beat a little faster and triggers that *fight or flight* reaction. It's physiological even more than psychological.

It is much like that jealous spouse issue, often referred to as *pathological or delusional jealousy*, or *Othello Syndrome*. One partner has a deep-rooted distrust and projects in numerous ways upon the other. Often, it is jealousy related to fidelity, but it spans a variety of concerns in a relationship. It could be financial distrust, lack of intimacy, or even a fear of co-parenting. At the base of all of it, however, is a deeply rooted wound in the accusing partner - but the impact can be fatal.

There you are, at dinner with your spouse, and he makes eye contact with a well-dressed woman. Immediately, the jealousy flairs. Was he flirting with her? Can you be certain? You ask him about the gaze, and he explains that she looked familiar – like someone his brother used to date.

The accusation starts a dinner-wrecking argument. While the argument fades over the next few days, you can't help but notice that he has not offered another night out, however.

Possible reasons:

- Scenario 1: He was guilty of eyeing the other woman and is afraid of being caught again.

- Scenario 2: The accusation was inaccurate, but the inference has now created a rift – for no reason at all.

Arguably, both scenarios are rooted in the issue of trust, and a lack of trust will shake the fabric of any relationship. If scenario 1 were accurate, shame on him. But if scenario 2 were accurate, a problem was created for absolutely no reason. Not only has it caused this week's argument, but it has also planted a seed of distrust in the relationship that was left unresolved.

The trail of consequences is endless once we begin journeying down that wormhole.

- He feels disrespected by her accusation, so he withdraws his affection.
- She feels unlovable, so she quits affirming him.
- He feels disrespected by her lack of affirmation, so he further withdraws his affection.

It's a viscous cycle, honestly, and one that is explained best in Dr. Emerson Eggerichs' book *Love and Respect*. And, while I believe this may be too obvious to even write, once trust is broken, it never fully heals. It leaves some dent or crack in the foundation which will always remain.

Each member of a team must feel safe. Their insecurities should be valued and protected. Their fears should always be validated, and their opinions should always be heard.

"The best way to find out if you can trust somebody is to trust him."

- Ernest Hemingway

PERSONAL CONFESSION

Building on my confession from the last chapter (you'll recall the girl who left the hotel while I was in the shower), you can call this "part two." Same girl, same issues, all rooted in an inexhaustible case of jealousy

(But first, let me state that I have never been unfaithful in a relationship. I have too much respect for myself, much less the other person.)

I continue this story, not to revisit her unfounded jealousy, but to acknowledge the people who are impacted by the dysfunction. Because of the commotion that always seemed to exist, I became distanced from some of my closest friends. Acknowledging her insecurities, I kept the strictest of boundaries and still couldn't seem to meet muster. I would leave my phone in the car if we went to a restaurant. I would never post on social media. I wouldn't even reply to text messages from female friends or coworkers for fear it would cause an argument. Heck, I remember one fight because my *dad* was texting me one day.

The part that was the most damaging wasn't what it did to *our* relationship (hell, that dumpster fire was already ablaze), it was the damage it did to the relationships around us. People were afraid of contacting *me*. People stopped wanting to spend time with *us*. The fallout was terrible. Years later, I have relationships with friends which have never been the same. Once that distance sets in, it seldom goes back to normal.

By not mastering this issue of trust, I allowed decay to set in throughout other areas of my life, the consequences of which can be still felt – ten years later. Not resolving this one key issue became an insidious cancer in many different relationships. And, while I could talk for hours about the importance of being a genuine version of yourself, it can suffice to say that living in a guarded, fearful relationship bleeds into all areas quickly.

The one thing she wanted most desperately was emotional intimacy, but her inability to trust caused her to lose the greatest gift she ever could have had (yes, I laughed while writing that).

From the CEO's Desk

As this chapter is flowing from my fingers, I remember this one young fella who worked for me some years back. Super nice guy. Fashionista, for sure. Early in his time with us, however, his integrity was tested (quite on accident).

In a meeting, I asked him to review a document I had sent to him that morning. I asked him to comment on it and see how it could be used in an upcoming campaign. He acknowledged receipt.

The following week, I had asked how things were coming along and he confirmed that he had been working on the rewrite. Great.

The following week, I made another inquiry regarding the status and was told that it was taking longer than planned, but he was making progress.

The following week, I asked about the delay and was told that he was nearly finished, but it was "making a lot more sense now."

The following week, I was asked to forward the document to another staff member, yet when I reviewed my sent items, I realized that I had forgotten the original attachment.

Week after week, he continued to lie about the project. He never received the document, yet acted as if he did. (I mean, how does that end well?)

When questioned, he apologized for the lie, asking for another chance. And while the second chance was granted, the distrust made the working relationship very complicated. His word had no value to me, nor to anyone else who knew of the situation.

Once that trust is broken, everything is suspect.

RYZE-ING TO THE OCCASION

Recently, we interviewed a nice young girl, and she asked the obvious question about vacation and sick days – "especially in light of Covid," she added.

Honestly, I don't remember the last time we've talked about paid time off, as it never seems to be an issue around our place.

I replied: "We have a policy manual in place that outlines our allowable sick and vacation time policies – making no exception for Covid. I will add, however, that my goal is to never have to enforce any of those policies because we can trust our entire staff to not abuse our willingness to overlook its existence."

Net in effect, we trust that our people are not going to abuse our flexibility. As such, we don't even track vacation or sick days. Once it gets taken advantage of, we will be forced to enforce the rules, but

I hope that day never comes.

Advice: Trust your people; they'll trust you back.

Today's Lessons Learned

- Trust is not easily given and even less easy to give again.
- The ripple effect that occurs when trust breaks down can lead to hidden consequences of which are not even aware.
- Distrust is the ugly stepmother of devalue. When people feel as if they are not trusted, it makes them feel as if they are not valued.
- If you are in any type of relationship and trust becomes an issue, address the root cause immediately.

Now, Ask Yourself

- Self, when you are feeling as if you should not trust someone, are there any other variables or behavioral cues that align? Do they remind you of someone else? Past offenses?
- Self, when you feel as if you should not trust someone, do you communicate that clearly and fairly?
- Self, when have you betrayed someone else's trust? Did you make it right and own your behavior?
- Self, why in the world would Mark stay in that relationship for so long?

On seeking approval.

CHAPTER 10: MEETING THE FAMILY

It's going to happen eventually, right? You get into this thing called "relationship" and – as much as it would be great to just keep it between the two of you (the way you're convinced nature intended) – you inherit the whole family. The *whole* family. Remember that fact, ladies and gentlemen, you are marrying the in-laws too. That alone should be enough to scare the be-jeezus out of any of us (especially anyone considering marrying me!).

So, here we are, a few months past that big first date. So far, it has been a lot of fun. You're learning each other's styles. Learning each other's preferences. Even learning each other's faults. But, soon thereafter, there comes a day that you must start interacting with more than just the significant other. Dating, after all, comes with intention. That intention leads to courtship. Courtship leads to marriage. And, along that road, you will encounter a fair number of characters. Sometimes it feels like you're Dorothy just trying to spend some quality time with the wizard, but the journey becomes jam packed with brainless, heartless, spineless add-ons – and maybe even a witch or two. (Good news, ladies, it may also come with a pair of killer heels, so think quick if a house comes flying your way.)

Here we go. First dinner with the family. Let's assume it's Thanksgiving or something, so the whole family is around. We'll make it extra scary. This is, after all, a foreshadowing of what all holidays will look like – 'til death do you part. Prepare for takeoff. (I can't help picturing some scene from a National Lampoon's movie – including Cousin Eddie.)

You really want to make a good impression here, but you're obviously nervous. You're shaking. You're clammy. Palms sweaty. Mom's spaghetti. (I'm from Detroit. I can't help it.)

First impressions matter, so we've learned, so you're on your best behavior. Then comes the firing squad.

"So, how did you meet?"

"When's the wedding?"

"I like you better than the last guy."

Or maybe, "What are your intentions with my daughter?"

You've been working for the last few months to earn the heart of your one true love, but now it feels like you're starting from square one. And as the daylight fades to night, the gauntlet grows more intense.

Before we get too far into the holiday cheer though, let's set some groundwork for our professional juxtaposition. Just like everything we have done so far, let's talk about how this "meet the family" moment parallels much of the way we must deal with our clients and other professional relationships. Dear, God, it's nearly a direct parallel, so I'd be a fool to not call this one out quickly.

Professionally, you know the moment. You're new to the account and you have a single contact at the client's firm. So far, the entire relationship has been mostly "onboarding." Things are looking positive. You guys have gotten along just fine and you both seem eager to take things to the next level.

Being in a business which demands that I meet a lot of people on a regular basis, I find myself making some fast connections. You know the type. Those people you meet, and it feels like you've known them for a hundred years. You talk about business opportunities, and it just feels like you're going to be BFFs. It nearly feels like a professional romance; things just feel so perfect.

Here I am picking out wallpaper and China patterns, and then comes my favorite line: "I can't wait to introduce you to my _____."

Maybe it's the CEO. Maybe the vice president of marketing. Maybe the business partner. Hell, it might as well be the receptionist, because now I'm having to "resell" myself to someone else. And, if that person(s) doesn't love me just as much, this relationship could be taking a very drastic turn. All I know is, someone just got invited to my party and this romance just started to feel like a negotiation.

So, what gives? Here we are, ready to sign the contract, make the deal, and now someone else must chime in? I'm back in sales mode – again. [grumbles]

Been there? Yeah, me too.

I remember a time when this happened to me – *vividly*. My contact was the COO of a relatively large business. We clicked instantly.

My time with him was all sunshine. The marketing director was all in too. What I didn't know was that the CEO called all of the shots. (A detail they failed to share.)

I had already pulled out my best work and was left feeling like I had exhausted all "my moves." Now I must impress someone else? (As I'm all about efficiency, all I could think was, "Why didn't you just introduce me to him first?")

As crazy as this may sound, it felt like I was "meeting the parents." I was coached in advance of the meeting and told what to expect, how to best communicate, what answers would be most impressive … like I was about to have Thanksgiving dinner with the family.

Throughout the meeting, I was even getting some non-verbal affirmations and quick head nods from the team.

Questions flew (many I had already answered in previous meetings).

My favorite: "What does [name omitted to protect the innocent] see in you?"

It wasn't so much an insult as it was a business owner asking a direct question. His question, better phrased: "What unique selling proposition made my team feel you were the best option?"

What I heard: "Why would my daughter want to marry you?"

You see, the question is all the same. It's all about acceptance. And to quote an anonymous source, "It takes a village." Truly. When you find "the one," you need to be ready to prove it to everyone.

So, how do you know the balance between "loving the one you're with" and "meeting the parents"? Well, Focker, I'd love to tell you it's going to be easy, but it isn't.

Red Pill Day

All families are crazy. Let's just be real. And when you meet someone who tells you that his family isn't crazy ... well, you have just met a liar. Why am I so confident in saying that? Because I speak cold, hard truth, my friend. There is no conceivable way, IMHO (note how youthful and hip I am using text code), that a random group of people with totally dissimilar interests can possibly converge annually on each national holiday and not cause some form of global decay. Statistically, I'll argue that it is impossible.

But, crazy or otherwise, we all have them, albeit some are worse than others.

Curiously, not everyone knows that their families are crazy yet. I have encountered folks who still believe that their families are very normal – as if nobody has broken the news to them yet.

Do you remember the moment you found out your family was crazy? Seriously, like in a total Alice in Wonderland, Matrix-style moment, a la Laurence Fishburne, complete with red and blue pills, you were faced with the bitter truth that you are the member of a dysfunctional micro-society of genetically-homogenous cyborgs, each designed with state-of-the-art, built-in Freudian-like ego defense systems. If it ever happened, you'd remember it.

I'm going somewhere with this, but I remember, about 141 years ago, when a friend courteously let me know that my family wasn't normal. I laugh just remembering the moment. Right smack dab in the middle of a conversation, she looked at me with a very puzzled look, as if she just realized that I had missed some kind of social cue and wanted to ensure that I was keeping up with the rest of the world.

"Marcus," she said (my friends call me "Marcus"), "You *do* know your family is crazy, right?" That plainly. That "out there."

In the middle of a story about God-knows-what, she just interrupted me, mid-sentence, and declared the most profound truth anyone had ever been bold enough to share with me. And the funniest part about the whole conversation was that I just stopped talking. I had no idea how to process this brand-new information.

My family is crazy? That's not normal? Other people don't do things like that? You mean to say that not everybody's family is like this? I could go through the epically-dysfunctional thoughts that followed, but I'll restrain myself from doing so - "because I care." Suffice to say, however, it was an epiphany.

I call it my "red pill day." It was the day that I was willing to accept that I needed a psychological reorganization. I needed to revisit *a lot* of things and begin to refilter them through this new lens. It was so profound, honestly, but the best part of the entire experience was that I was never able to go back to seeing the world the same way again.

And, welcomed or otherwise, I suddenly felt responsible to tell everyone else that their families were crazy too! (For the sake of the reader, I'll spare you the experience of attempting the same and warn you that most people don't welcome that news.)

WE ALL HAVE THEM

Every man or woman you will ever date *also* has a family. And, as you could expect, they're crazy too. It's a jungle out there, friends. Two people fall in love, decide that they could potentially do life together, and then spend the rest of their lives trying to convince everyone else why this is a good decision. I think a lot of potentially good relationships die trying to earn the approval of what I refer to as the "buying committee." Some unsolicited "audience participation" keeps a good thing from ever becoming great.

The opinions of those we love weigh heavily on our relationships.

I remember taking this one girl to a dinner with my aunt and uncle once. I thought she was great, but within moments of the dinner beginning, she made some comment that my aunt found inappropriate. It was relatively innocent, in retrospect, but when she excused herself to the ladies' room, my aunt commented to my uncle, "I wonder what rock he found her under."

[moment of silence]

Wait! Scratch that. No moment of silence. Looking back on that relationship, kudos to Auntie for seeing it early!

But the point is, the family's opinion matters. And, before you get your panties wadded up in your "*other people's opinions don't matter to me*" bunch, just stick with me here: It changes things. No matter who you are. No matter who they are. No matter how much you try to minimize it. It matters.

In every relationship, there is a buying committee, whether personal or professional. I'm not saying I like it. I'm just saying that it is true. Our tribal origins require that new members must be vetted. And only acceptance from the tribe will justify entry.

So, get used to the crowd, my friend. You're marrying the in-laws too.

Personal Confession

I remember one of the most painful "trying to fit in" stories I can remember. I have a cousin. Fun person, although a bit jilted in her own right, but for a time, she was cool. Quite funny, with a completely unfiltered sense of humor.

Well, she started dating this ... guy. (See how the disapproval starts?) I mean, nice enough guy but sweet baby Jesus, I have never seen anyone want to fit in so badly. I suppose it was well-intentioned, but it couldn't have been more awkward.

Now, in fairness, meeting my family is like entering a den of wolves, so I cut the guy some slack. But here he is, nice, blue-collar, beta male and he showed up to a family event with a house full of alphas. Arguably, his worst nightmare, but he aimed to impress.

The irony of the entire thing is that the guy is the perfect likeness to Paul Blart, mall cop. You know the guy: Kevin James' character who rides a Segway through the shopping mall to protect citizens from petty crime. You can't make this stuff up. I couldn't even remember his name for the longest time because I could only call him "Paul Blart." (To add to the joke, he worked in the safety department of a manufacturing facility and all he ever talked about was plant safety.) Yet, for my cousin's sake, I bit my tongue. And, as far as "Paul" knew, we were friends, because I wasn't going hurt my cousin.

Sometime later, in a completely random conversation, I accidentally referred to him by his nickname in front of my cousin. We all froze, worried how she would react. After all, it was a jab at her would-be husband.

She nearly died laughing. She found it so funny, in fact, that she couldn't wait to tell him, convinced he would find it hilarious (really, the resemblance was uncanny, so she may have been right).

We never learned much about how their conversation went, but when we saw him the next day, his mustache was gone. Legit. It may seem like nothing more than the loss of a lip caterpillar, but I felt horrible.

To him, our opinion was so important. He felt that if we didn't approve, she would end the relationship, so he worked tirelessly to earn the buying committee's blessing.

(Also, sadly, attempting to keep up with family vacations and holiday traditions, he buried them in debt, rather than admit they couldn't afford to join. Sad.)

From the CEO's Desk

Sometimes "meeting the family," in business allegory, is a bit more complicated than you may think – like when the buying committee doesn't even know you're coming to dinner. (I strongly recommend avoiding surprises at this point of the game.)

Setting the stage here, I was recently asked if I would be interested in a client referral. I did some quick research on the client and learned that they were a perfect fit for our agency. I wasn't given much information about the current situation but figured I would receive something of a debrief and a warm handoff. After all, it was a referral and those typically flow quite smoothly.

[crickets]

Then, one afternoon, I was copied on an email which read more like a breakup letter between the other two companies.

Oh, sweet Moses, what is happening?

Assuming there must have been other conversations preceding this abrupt "introduction," I *replied all* with some congenial language about my exuberance for the brand and the project, hoping to break the ice.

[crickets]

Some time passed and I reached out to the CMO (who I had known from a previous life, coincidentally). Turns out, he was just as surprised by the abrupt assignment of contract (turns out it was not a referral, in the traditional sense of the word).

[crickets]

Here I am, "invited to family dinner," but nobody told the buying committee that it was coming. The CEO and the CFO had no idea who I was, nor did they know that their prior agent was planning to exit their agreement.

I was invited to "meet the family," but the family did not know they were meeting me. So, here I am, practically sitting in a folding chair with a mismatched dinner plate, trying to make room between two other place settings at the dining room table – the clumsy "add on" that nobody knew was joining the festivities.

The lesson: Never show up unannounced to these types of events. It's really awkward when you're the only guy at the table with a nametag. It's hard to impress someone when the only question they're asking is "who are you again?"

Ryze-ing to the Occasion

Our clients are profoundly diverse. Although they are mostly in the natural health and beauty space, they are entrepreneurs and are constantly in need of nurturing and care. No offense to any clients, past or present, but we are what we are. As business owners, we want attention – urgently.

Well, at our place, we have found a way to stratify our contacts with clients, matching each member of the client's team with an appropriate title from our own team. We try to keep *like things* in *like places*.

As an example, as the CEO, I try to keep my direct communication limited to other CEOs and business owners. I will seldom ever join a conference call unless the business owner is joining as well. Scheduled calls with the client's marketing director, for instance, are managed by our director of accounts or our vice president of operations. I'm always available, of course, but I find the conversations are unevenly matched when I'm present.

When I'm speaking to an entrepreneur or CEO, we have similar goals and even similar nomenclature. We look for big picture strategies and strategize together. We focus on relationship.

When my operations team is on a call, they're talking about transactional things (things I would rather not engage, honestly). The client's marketing director or customer service manager is asking operational questions, and those are best answered by people who are focused on the same types of transactions.

The goal is to keep the conversation balanced.

Imagine with me the day on which you and your partner's families first met each other. Naturally, the dads started talking to each other. The moms gravitated to each other. The conversations flowed more naturally (well, I hope so for your sake) because the individuals were equally assigned to their counterparts.

And, let's be honest, if I were on every call, I'd sound like the cranky grandpa who was sitting at the kids' table. It's best for everyone.

Today's Lessons Learned

- In any relationship, there is a buying committee. Be prepared.
- Everyone's family is crazy. It's part of the game.
- Selling yourself and your value, whether personally or professionally, never stops. As the audience changes, the message must be repeated.
- Paul Blart is a hero.

Now, Ask Yourself

- Self, when were you last disappointed because you thought you had made a good impression, only to be surprised?
- Self, when making relationship decisions, do you consider the buying committee, or do you devalue their input?
- Self, who is on your buying committee and how much does their opinion weigh into your relational decisions?
- Self, how do you prepare others when they are about to meet your buying committee? Do you balance their opinions properly?

On balancing expectations.

CHAPTER 11: MOVING IN TOGETHER
(and other common law pit falls)

Recently, a friend and I were having a conversation and a phrase was thrown around that made me laugh (maybe a bit of a guilty laugh, but a laugh nonetheless).

She said, "It's like marriage, really." (Don't ask me what we were talking about. I really don't remember.) "Men assume that the women they marry will never change. And women figure that men will change as soon as they get married."

Ouch. Talk about some expectation fails.

Been there? You know what I mean then.

Before the wedding, she's always perfect hair and makeup. She loves everything he loves and makes a point of showing affection without expectation. She knows how to give him space - *and* keep him coming back for more. After all, she knew how to make him want to buy that ring. Something worked.

Meanwhile, she's secretly hoping that his "bachelor habits" are short-lived, and that he'll, perhaps, grow up a bit once marriage brings out the maturity in him. He's just a boy, she figures, but she'll help make him a man.

You can laugh, but you know it's truer than most women would care to admit. Not for *you*, of course, but for someone you know. (Like the movie *American Pie*. If you didn't identify with one of the characters, you knew someone who could – which made it that much funnier.) She wanted to date boys, but she wanted to marry a man.

Meanwhile, somewhere in Neverland, Peter Pan is excited that this girl is cool with all his habits. He is playing his games and shaving only on Mondays – and she's totally cool with it. Buy her a ring and you can get away with anything, he figures. She's beautiful. Always looks great. He's in sweatpants; she's in heels. What could go wrong?

Then it happens. Move-in day. Whether married or otherwise, nothing exposes a person's true self like cohabitating. Love notes and midnight texts turn into toilet seat outbursts and stray socks. Crazy how that happens so fast.

Enjoy this compilation of reasons women complain about living with men. It has been well-researched, so don't question the guru.

1. He always relies on me to do everything.
2. He doesn't even know what's going on half the time.
3. It's always the same argument, repeatedly.
4. He drinks too much. (Hell, I started drinking, just reading numbers 1-3.)
5. The budget seems to always be a surprise.
6. He doesn't appreciate anything I do.
7. I have to teach him basic skills.
8. He gives me the silent treatment when he's mad.
9. He's never around anymore.
10. I can't seem to do anything right.

Ouch. Maybe "enjoy" was too strong of a word. I think it would be hard for anyone to *enjoy* that list – for *any* reason. But there is always another side to the story.

What do men complain about?

1. She's changed. Nothing pleases her anymore.

2. She doesn't give me any space of my own.
3. She never says what she means.
4. The end.

Not hard to imagine that the list is shorter for men (NOTE: I abridged the original list for women from 20 things. You're welcome.)

Moving in changes everything. It's that moment when all the courting rituals take a hiatus and the gloves come off. Best behavior is no longer necessary, it would seem, because the deal has been sealed. There is this common law sense of comfort that begins to set in – or just bubble beneath the surface. And it doesn't matter how "good things are," you know what I mean.

With stars in their eyes, couples the world over sign up for this modern-day shackling, and are always surprised when things aren't as romantic as they pictured (see the lists above). But don't let me throw shade on your nuptial parade. Try it and see how it goes. Really.

In all seriousness though, nothing is more exciting than when you are in perfect harmony and lockstep with your significant other. Great things happen when selfless people combine forces toward a common goal. I was reading a quote the other day that I thought was profound:

"Marriage was never meant to be a power struggle. It was meant to be a power union."

Likely, you're grown up enough to know what it feels like to cohabitate, even with a roommate (or maybe you're still sharing a bedroom with a sibling), so you understand the good and the bad of it. You understand the highs and the lows, and you have enough experience to get through the stupid spats and the petty bickering. I hope.

Now, let's flow seamlessly to our regularly scheduled juxtaposition.

During the early days of client relationships, or even business partnerships, things are great. You can never foresee a problem. You just see everything the same. You're excited for the future. The contracts aren't necessary, right? Because no two people could ever have been more in agreement than the two of you.

Now, if there's anything I've learned in business (and any lesson I care to share with you), it is that humans suck.

Write that down right here in the margin. I'll leave you some space.

Humans. Suck. Write it.

    Humans. →

    Suck. →

Don't believe me? Log onto Facebook quickly and tell me about the first ten posts that you see, noting that on Facebook, these are all humans who you have *chosen* to have in your life (well, your fake life).

With little exception, I'd guess that nothing you see there is anything you needed to hear today. In fact, I would say that only one of those posts is by someone who you would call a real-life friend. Hate talk. Ads. Whining. Politics. BLAH! Unwelcomed garbage in your life.

But, let me say this: They haven't done anything wrong. We can groan all day about the content we were fed on that social media thread, but nobody did anything that wasn't perfectly permissible (or perfectly fact-checked).

The disconnect? The expectations.

I scroll social media to keep up with the people I don't see often, or maybe find some wickedly funny memes. Some clever humor. Yet, when I begin reading, I am usually inundated with messages which aim to trigger my emotions using politics, puppies, and a variety of other pandemonium.

When I engaged my social media feed today, I had an expectation of what I would find there. When fed these other messages, my expectations were disappointed, and I disengaged.

But what does this have to do with moving in together?

It's all about the expectations. What you expect from the other person is the violation. You *expect* things, then they are violated. Why? Because they were never discussed in advance. You just assumed.

Just. Like. Business.

Every client I have ever courted, or every partnership I have ever indulged, came to me with expectations of how I was *supposed to do things*. Sometimes it is just a matter of communication style. Sometimes it is the expectation of profit-sharing. Sometimes it is the nuances of an operating agreement. The trouble is that these items are seldom discussed in advance. They are assumed. It is just expected that the rest of the world functions the same way that I do. So many unspoken rules, all craving to be violated more than a … I'll just stop there. (There is no way to finish that sentence with dignity, so I'll just preserve what little I have left and move on.)

In a previous life, I was a member of the academic community (let that sink in, if you will … I'll laugh along). We would often discuss the topic of "how expectations shape perception." And, when engaging a student population, I would frequently find myself the arbiter of these expectations. Expectations, after all, are "prior beliefs." And prior beliefs are based on "prior experiences."

Concisely, the way I view the present is quite usually tied to the way I *experienced* the past.

Our sense of "fairness" is usually a result of what we have experienced. In life, we tend to expect a lot of the same. We're not offended by the same. Why do privileged people expect better service? Because they're accustomed to it. Why do underprivileged people not seem to be offended by bad service? Because they're accustomed to it. You can call me pretentious, but I call it "conditioned."

Enter a new business partner.

You bring with you years of experiences. He/she brings the same years of *different* experience. Neither of you spend time discussing your expectations. They're expectations, after all. The speed at which you answer your phone is not outlined in the contract, but it better be as fast as he expects you to answer.

Before the ink is even dry, it seems like each party finds reasons to rip the contract in half as dramatically as Nancy Pelosi at a State of the Union speech. And nobody did anything wrong. Likely, you just moved in together before you were ready.

Then, you ask, how can you be ready? There must me a way to overcome this hurdle, wise one. Show me your ways!

Ahh, yes. I will, my student.

Details.

Nothing about the details is sexy. I mean, nothing.

There you are, lying in bed (we have moved from the business metaphor just in case you didn't track). You and your beloved decide that "it's time." It's scary. It's exciting. It's a big step, for sure, but the deal gets sealed without so much as a conversation about shared responsibilities, laundry, finances, alarm clocks, groceries, or where we spend the holidays. That's just taboo talk while lying in bed still. You can't talk about those things without clothes on, after all. The universe may disown you.

So, naked as a jaybird, you agree to break your lease and put your life into upheaval without so much as a whisper about who is going to park in the garage (it should be her, after all; she's the girl, right?). Expectations.

Your clients aren't any different, by the way. The devil is always in the details.

I have had multi-million-dollar deals get sealed over dinner with a handshake and no contract. Foolish as it may sound, it "just felt right." And, if someone had started talking about contracts and getting my attorney involved, it would have just killed the mojo. You start fearing that if we talk about valuations and exit strategies that the deal may never get off the ground.

So, you settle for "I'll cross that bridge when I get there."

No.

No, no, no.

No, no, no, no, NO!

Bridges all get crossed now.

Before taking that "no way back" road trip, you map the infrastructure.

What do we do in the event of a disagreement? How do we settle complaints? What is the cancelation policy? Is there a minimum expectation of performance? How do we measure success? How is success, *in excess of expectation*, rewarded?

Just this month, I have encountered these situations a minimum of four times.

- Two weeks ago, while talking to a potential business partner, he was asking questions and kept apologizing for asking so many questions about an operating agreement. My response: "Do not apologize. It is always easier talking about these things *before* we are in the heat of battle. It lets us be objective. Part of hammering out an operating agreement is having to talk through all of the tough scenarios – before they become a reality."

- Last week, I had a video call with a current business partner on our recent launch. With a super tight operating agreement in place, we talked through increased, unforeseen costs of goods. Because of the way we work, and our business is structured, we were able to have a very productive conversation about a "way forward" despite the costs. We have a mature partnership.

- Last night, I had a client emailing me about contract clarifications. She asked, "Can we make the term of the contract month-to-month, rather than a six-month minimum." Politely, I declined the request. "You see, our work is all front-loaded on this engagement. We need six months to even break even on our initial onboarding. If you can't risk six months, I can't risk the first month either."

- This morning, I woke up to an email from an overseas business partner (more on him later). He was asking about details regarding the dissolution of our partnership. The problem: There are no details because he never put anything in an operating agreement. He left all the power on my side of the pond. Not that I would be dishonest with him, but foolish move to give away your power simply because you were too busy to write things down.

I'll tell you a secret: There is no cure in existence that is better than an ounce of prevention. In a past life as a college professor, I remember talking to my students about their class projects (their dream business plans). They were so sold that their plans were going to work – if only because they *wanted* them to work – that they ignored some gaping holes in the architecture. They became emotionally attached to the plan and naively would have invested their futures in plans that made no fiscal sense.

My advice, quite often, was not something they wanted to hear – but needed to. "The best written business plans," I would explain, "are those which warn you of an unwise decision." Sadly, there is this belief that you can just keep adjusting it until it works.

News flash: *Sometimes it just doesn't work.*

Just like dating.

Personal Confession

This one hurts to share, but I promised to be honest.

Once upon a time, I recall sitting with a premarital counselor discussing pending nuptials. During one session, I began to understand relationships as never before.

Here we are, happy in love, simply "checking the box" on premarital counseling (because that's what you do, so they say). I'm not sure I believed it mattered, but I played along and spent the time and the money.

Dear, Lord, was it well-spent.

The counselor, a man we had both known for years, was happy to work with us and discuss our upcoming marriage. I think he believed it was going to be an easy time, given his familiarity. He asked a lot of questions, as you would expect, mostly related to our relationship with each other. We must have passed all the tests, because everyone was still smiling. Until it happened.

The counselor pulled out this interesting matrix-like diagram. He asked us two questions and then we were told to plot our answers on this chart. The chart used an x-y matrix to measure *closeness* and *flexibility* within the family unit (i.e., how much involvement family has in each other's lives and how rigid are the rules).

- Question 1: "Using the matrix, where would you plot your family of origin? Are they overly involved in each other's lives or detached? Are they flexible in structure or military in their compliance with family rules?"

- Question 2: "Now, on the same chart, can you please indicate where you believe a family should be? After all, you're starting a new family of your own; where will you fall on this matrix?"

I remember my answers quite well. My family was *way too* involved and *way too* flexible during my upbringing. My expectation was that my new family (our family) would be more balanced in both areas (less family involvement and a little more structure). The counselor acknowledged how I recognized past dysfunction and seemed to understand the need for balance. (Recognized it? It practically lurked under my bed and scared me awake every night!)

Then came the moment of truth when my betrothed revealed her answers. Her family of origin was *way too* involved and *way too* flexible too, much like my own family. The counselor's quizzical look appeared, however, when he revealed that she plotted our future family at the exact same intersection. I was stunned.

Translated: She didn't think that her family was dysfunctional at all (she needed to read chapter 10). And, even worse, it meant that her *expectations* were that *our* family would function the same way (well, *dys*-function the same).

All along, we had recognized how similar our families were. Foolishly, we saw this as a strength – a bond. Turns out we didn't see it the same after all. It was like we found kinship in our addictions, but only one of us was in recovery! Very, very different expectations. 'Nuff said.

I read a quote recently, but do not remember the source. It read: "*Stop mistaking shared trauma for compatibility.*" Let that sink in.

From the CEO's Desk

A few pages back, I mentioned a conversation with a business partner in which we drilled through every terrible possibility-imaginable problem which could ever arise in our venture. We wrote exit strategies and performance expectations and everything. We were mature enough to have difficult conversations before anything could go wrong.

Later, trouble arose. Specifically, I was going to move forward with a marketing strategy with which he didn't agree. It wasn't so much of an argument, as it was a priority issue about where to spend available cash.

Fortunately, we had a source document to refer back to. We each had done our best to get the other on board with our respective reasoning, but to no avail. At the end of the conversation, I was able to say: "Since we can't seem to come to an agreement, let's consult our operating agreement and see what it says."

The operating agreement stated that marketing decisions were wholly mine, so we were able to agree that we were moving forward.

I heard him out and took his opinion under advisement, but because we had expectations drawn out in advance, there was no rift in the relationship at all. We honored our agreement and there were no hard feelings over it (no feelings at all, in fact, because it was spelled out in black and white).

For the record, the marketing plan was a huge success! Thanks, @DaveAsprey. ;)

Ryze-ing to the Occasion

It has become a joke around our office that any time a person comes in to interview, "[I] will do everything in [my] power to convince the person to *not* work with us." It may be true.

I simply start every interview with something like, "before we start asking questions about you, I want to tell you a bit about us ... the good and the bad." By the time I'm done airing all our dirty laundry and internal shortcomings, we expect most people to run for the hills. If they don't, then we keep the interview going.

Why do I do this? Because too often, I hear people talking about the potential position as being some kind of mythical lottery ticket. As if getting this job will make all of your wildest dreams come true. Then, once the employee resigns from their old position and moves into the new role, they are stunned to find out the truth about their decision. Sure, we're a great team with some great potential for new hires, but we're flawed and stressful and can be somewhat disorganized too.

We're not trying to trick people into joining our team. We want people who know exactly what they're getting into ... the good and the bad. We want people who fit our culture and want to make us better.

We set expectations – good and bad.

(P.S. – Nothing is a greater turnoff than a resume which reads "looking to gain experience ..." For Peter's sake, please lie to me.

Don't explain how you're going to use us. Tell me how you're going to add value *here*.)

Today's Lessons Learned

- Often, avoiding disappointment in the future is a function of setting expectations in the present.
- Setting expectations is not sexy or romantic, but solid relationships are built on being able to plan a future together.
- In business, and likewise relationships, discovering pitfalls early can save you from long-term heartache.
- Your expectations will never completely match someone else's, but if you plan for the differences, they don't become fatal.

Now, Ask Yourself ...

- Self, do you avoid talking about negative things for fear that it will bring present-day conflict?
- Self, when your expectations are not fulfilled, how do you usually react? Do you defend? Do you compromise? Do you retreat?
- Self, do you recall a time when you could have avoided certain heartaches by talking before acting?
- Self, how could you begin safeguarding your current relationships by setting expectations even now?

On sharing appreciation.

CHAPTER 12: FRIDAY NIGHT IS DATE NIGHT
(Subtitled: Try a Little Tenderness)

I have an embarrassing story to tell here. And, over halfway through this novella, you shouldn't be surprised that I have an embarrassing story to tell. What should surprise you is that I am calling this one an embarrassing story and have just talked about the rest like they are part of everyday life. This one must be impressive, right? Strangely, until sitting down to write this chapter, the connection never occurred to me, but it also birthed the subtitle.

Some years back (an unfortunate number of years), I was dating this girl who I was simply crazy about. So much chemistry. So much playfulness. So much "spark," we'll say. She was the kind of girl who got noticed. Bubbly. Fun. Always saw the good things about life. Yet, somehow, I managed to bring out the worst in her. I mean, I could make this girl cry like nothing you've ever seen. (And, before you go all "high and mighty," it wasn't because I was trying to make her cry, jack-o. That's the point of the story.) I mean, we were so compatible in so many ways, but the tears. My precious Lord in heaven, the tears. Like south Florida in the summer, I could set my watch to the predictable showers that would fall – nearly daily.

I kept thinking to myself: "This isn't normal. There is something wrong with her. Something very, very wrong."

And perhaps that's true (sorry if you're actually reading this, but you come out like the hero in this one), but this left-brained cyborg (me) wasn't following this trail of tears.

One day, and I remember it well, I realized that I was *100%* right. (Of note, gentlemen, this is never true. Ever. There does not exist a reality in which you are ever 100% right. To paraphrase Doctor Strange in the Marvel Comic movie *Infinity Wars*, "Out of 14,000,605 potential future realities, there is only 1 chance to win this battle.")

I realized that everything that would get her upset was related to things that I *never* did. Here I am thinking of all the things that I did right, and she would always see the things I *didn't* do. Not doing something right, for the record, is much different than doing something wrong. And, in the world of male-female relationships, so I've learned the hard way, men tend to keep score of the things that *happened*, while women keep score by the number of opportunities *missed*. Like in a hockey game, gents, you not only track the number of goals scored, but also the ratio of goals to shots on goal.

Well, I figured out the perfect way to solve the problem (also a favorite of women, if you're taking notes: they love being "solved"). Oy vey!

Dipping back into my days in clinical psychology, I suggested (read as "insisted") that she and I both take a Myers-Briggs Type Indicator (MBTI). In doing so, I could show her, empirically, how we were seeing the world so drastically different, and would, thus, solve her emotions. Voila!

Here's me: ENTP.

Here's her: ENFJ.

Now, if you know anything about the MBTI, those two middle letters are *really, really* important. But, let me translate, just in case you're not up to speed on your personality test results.

According to the MBTI, an "N" is an intuitive person, meaning that we tend to see the world *as it isn't*. We think very abstractly, rather than concretely. We imagine and invent and problem solve and find ways that things *could be* done, rather than being limited by space and time and those overrated five senses. Well, that's the way an "NT" (me) sees the world (the "T" being a *thinker*).

Insert "NF" (her) for comparison.

According to the MBTI, an "F" is a person who tends to process information *first* through emotion. Not to say that they are emotional, but they *feel* information before inserting the logic (exactly the opposite of their "NT" counterparts). These folks, *bless their hearts*, imagine and dream and find ways that things *could have felt better*. If an emotion ranks as a 7, they see all the ways that it could have been an 8. Or a 9. Or a 10. Or, in this girl's case (whose world would always be filled with butterflies and calorie-free cupcakes if she could will it to be so), how it could rank as a 15.

Two largely embarrassing issues here:

1. I failed to recognize the unique perspective that she brought to the relationship, because things are right or wrong in my world. I saw that I did a lot of things and did them well. I failed to recognize that there were things that I could have done – and didn't. And I failed to see that she, like me, saw the world abstractly, but through the lens of emotion, rather than logic.

2. My dumb ass made her take a personality test. But it didn't stop at just taking the test. I went through her results and highlighted all the lines that proved my point and emailed them back to her to show her that nothing was wrong and that she was just being irrationally emotional about things that never happened.

It is at this point in the book that I feel as if I need to leave a few blank pages for you to jot down some notes of shameful disapproval which can be mailed to me in retribution. I believe Dante wrote about a level of hell filled with people who were going to spend eternity proving a moot point. Today, it feels like a vision of my future.

So, here we are. You, judgmental and disappointed. Me, face dripping with egg. But we move on.

And how does all of this relate to Friday date nights? Well, I'm glad you asked.

No two people in the world see things the same. I don't care how "in tune" you are with each other; you see the world differently. For my musician friends, remember that there is only a half of a step between harmony and dissonance. And, if you don't keep those strings tightened, it's amazing how fast things will devolve.

You cannot force someone to see the world your way. (Besides, how boring would that be?) The unique qualities that you each bring to the relationship make the whole greater than the sum of the parts. It's how 1+1 can equal 3. Together, with unique perspectives, you can cover more ground and avoid more pitfalls. Perspectives, if not kept – well, in perspective – can begin to quickly look like differences though.

Which brings me back to Friday nights.

Friday nights are tune-up nights. They are designated times to just go back to the basics. They are times that we celebrate those perspectives and sacrifice our preferences to give the other a voice again. They are times that we agree to put the ugliness of life behind us and recommit that we value the other's viewpoint.

Friday nights are milestones. They are moments when you get to remind yourself (and your partner) of the reasons you're doing life together. With billions of people in the world, this is the one you chose (and the one who chose you back).

Friday nights are times to choose each other again.

Geez! I wish I were better at taking my own advice.

But, while that may sound like solid dating – or even marriage – advice, there is a real-world *Date Your Clients* comparison to be made here. I hope you caught it already.

In every single one of my client relationships, we have disagreed on something. We haggled over strategy. Sometimes we completely butted heads. After all, we have different perspectives. It's normal. It's healthy.

Them: They know their product and/or services better than anyone. They live and breathe this stuff.

Me: I understand marketing better than they ever will. I know consumers and how/why they buy.

Together, we have the potential to take over the world. Apart, we are either a product manufacturer who can't sell anything or a marketing genius with nothing to sell. Painful. And, yes, I just called myself a marketing "genius." Get over it.

For this reason, it is important to stop and celebrate the uniqueness that both you and the client bring to the relationship. You're stronger together. But you need Friday nights.

And, just in case you're a little slow here, I'm not literally talking about Friday nights (maybe). I'm talking about intentional times at which you and your clients must reconnect and celebrate your partnership.

For us, as an advertising agency, our moments usually happen best in person, as literal Friday nights are hard for long-distance relationships. So, we start memorializing our shared wins by always asking our clients to share their sales numbers with us. Those are ours to brag about too, after all. We get excited about positive reviews. We talk to each as people and – please be seated for this – sometimes we don't even talk about work! [gasps]

Truth. Sometimes I spend time with my clients *not* talking about work. We talk like people. Humans. Humans who are made for relationship. Humans who must not only trust the people with whom they march into battle, but humans who must *like* those people too.

We talk about cars. And travel. And politics (but only with clients who politically agree with me, of course). We talk about things that remind the other person that we are *people*.

With my entrepreneurial clients, sometimes we sit and gripe about the stress of being business owners. Sometimes we sit and laugh at the years we never thought we would survive.

Like a healthy marriage, we need to remember why we chose to do business together. And the only way we are ever going to take the time to memorialize this choice is to be intentional. We must remember that Friday nights need to be special. We need to designate times that we just talk and remember that we "like each other." People do business with people, after all. That's the beauty of business: it is all about relationships.

Look back at my earlier anecdote about the MBTI. Imagine what a client would do if I sent him or her a test and asked for the results so that I could prove how their perspective was invalid. OMG! My new business team would be lynching me outside the building – and rightfully so.

So, let me ask the million-dollar question: What are you doing to memorialize the relationship you have with your clients? I'm guessing you send a gift at Christmas (or whatever "holiday season" political correctness you write on the card), but what else? Is once a year enough? Is an anniversary dinner enough to keep your marriage alive and committed?

Think about it.

When was the last time that you intentionally made someone remember why he or she was in a relationship with you? Even a friendship? Or an employee? Every day, I *choose* to work with the people who work with me. Every day, they wake up and choose to work with me. Sure, paychecks are great, but there is no shortage of options in the world. And, just like your client is getting wooed by a competitor every day, everyone in your life has options. But they are choosing you. Ask yourself why. In fact, ask *them* why. And when you figure it out, *do more of that*.

One of the best pieces of advice I have ever received in life has become my mantra as it relates to relationships. Simply, I was dared to enter every engagement with the intention of letting the other party win. Literally, the advice was to "enter each engagement with utter unselfishness, as if your only goal were to serve the other person." When relationships exist in which you have no expectations of reciprocity, it is not only amazing the amount of good you are capable of enacting, but the amount of reciprocity which follows is earth-shattering. (Now, don't go trying to be unselfish so that you can be "selfish in disguise." It doesn't work that way.)

In business, find what makes your employees tick and serve their needs. You'll be shocked at how they want to perform better.

In marriage, find what makes your partner tick. What are his or her buttons? How can you satisfy him or her without any expectations in return?

In friendships, how can you be the friend who is unselfishly caring for others?

Are you a provider? Provide.

Are you a defender of the weak? Defend.

Are you a fence mender? Mend.

Do what you do for the benefit of all involved but make a point of memorializing the relationship. Either of you could end it at any time, but you haven't yet. That's a win. Celebrate it!

And, if I'm being frank, finding a new group of people who would put up with you isn't an easy chore; learn to keep the ones you have!

Personal Confession

We all have stories about the "days of quarantine," amiright? (Also, it is fascinating to me that "amiright" is actually in the dictionary now.)

Well, one of the best things that happened to me during the early part of 2020 was the rekindling of relationships that I hadn't nurtured in years. With way too much time on my hands, I made a conscious decision to find ways to invest in random people from my life's story – both past and present. Usually, it would manifest in the form of arbitrary text messages sent to various people, but the content of those messages was a little different than you may assume. I tried to avoid the usual "Hey there!" and "You up?" texts. Instead, I would try to send messages which were crafted to celebrate something about that person or fondly recall a memory we shared.

The messages would include such things as, "Just wanted to remind you how valuable your friendship has been to me over the years." Often, it would lead to conversations about how that person was struggling, either emotionally or financially, during the pandemic times. I was gifted the opportunity to offer help to so many people throughout that time. In some cases, people I hadn't seen (or even talked to) in ten or more years. Sometimes, these random engagements led me to learn that they were struggling to pay the rent. So, I got to pay the rent – and it was my honor. We celebrated our friendship – and I was able to do so by reminded these people how my affection for them is unselfish and sacrificial.

And here is the best part of that story: In some instances, I reached out to someone and was the recipient of the blessing. Sometimes, I would initiate the conversation and end up receiving messages back that *blew me away*. I was told countless times about how I was valued and often given specific reasons why that was true.

Win-win.

It was like COVID gifted me with several months of Friday nights. (How's that for making the best of a sh#tty situation?)

FROM THE CEO'S DESK

Many years back, I remember a particular client always causing a problem for our operations director. She would get so incensed by the ridiculous things he would do (and I'm not even going to get in the details, because he was honestly ridiculous). She would complain to me incessantly, practically begging me to stop him from calling her – even suggesting that we terminate our agreement with him.

For what seemed like an eternity, she would complain about this guy, until one day when she and I shared an honest conversation.

"You'll remember back in the early days of the business when we didn't have many clients and cash was always tight? That client trusted us. We were a small, inexperienced company, and he took a chance on us. For nearly a year, in fact, he paid your payroll, week after week, because of his billings. He was our largest client, unbeknownst to him, and although he was a pain in the butt, even back then, he continued to pay faithfully and kept us in business. And, for *that* reason alone, I will never terminate our relationship with him. I will always remain loyal to someone who was loyal to me."

She got it.

Ryze-ing to the Occasion

It is such a task to memorialize the good times with our clients nowadays. We get busy. We get lazy. We get preoccupied. And, frankly, we start to treat people the way we are treated by others.

But here, we won't accept mediocrity. We pride ourselves on having concierge-level service for all clients – without exception.

It is notoriously our habit of building personal relationships with our clients. We want to partner with them and make their lives easier. We do so in the ways in which we mitigate problems, predictively forecasting deficiencies, and even helping to write policies to provide better service to their customers.

In doing these things, we stop and celebrate our relationships with them in unique ways. Sometimes we send gifts which we know they'd love. Sometimes, it is just a thoughtful card. Periodically, it is a case of wine and a box of bath bombs (seriously). We take the time to get to know them and celebrate our relationship though.

It's who we are.

Today's Lessons Learned

- Each person, and each relationship, is unique and should be fostered as such. There is no broad brush for "managing" a relationship.
- Memorializing the good things about your relationships keeps both parties coming back for more.
- Perspectives, if not kept in perspective, can begin to quickly look like differences.
- The unique qualities that you each bring to the relationship make the whole greater than the sum of the parts.

Now, Ask Yourself

- Self, what relationships do I take for granted? How can I memorialize the value they add to my life?
- Self, when differences arise (and they will arise), do I focus on the difference, or find common ground in the similarities.
- Self, have you been taking your clients for granted? Remember that finding a new client is a lot harder than keeping a current client.
- Self, how do you usually express gratitude? How you prefer to be shown gratitude? Do they match? Usually.

PART III: The Moment of Truth

On resolving conflict.

CHAPTER 13: THE FIRST FIGHT

The world is a meme.

I'm hard-pressed to deny that these five words summarize my learning style as of late. I mean, I think it's a gift to glean wisdom from even the most intellectually numbing form of entertainment. Whatever. Judge me later. It's true though.

But really, you know how sometimes you see something as simple as a photo with a few words and you're like, "Holy sh#t! That's so true." Well, I had one of those moments recently, and it shall serve as our inspiration for this brilliant chapter on *first fights*. But first, some unrelated thoughts before we land this flight.

> CONFESSION: I am likely the world's biggest *Friends* fan. It's true. I'm almost ashamed of it, but if *Friends Trivia* was a jeopardy category, I'd own you. And for those of you who can relate, we will relive, together, an episode wherein Chandler and Monica experience their first fight. (NOTE: Chandler Bing is my spirit animal, so this one bears down on my soul.)

EPISODE TRANSCRIPT: THE ONE WITH THE KIPS

(After a weekend getaway which resulted in a lot of arguing, Chandler stops at Monica's apartment.)

Chandler: Hey.

Monica: Hi.

Chandler: I just came over to drop off ... well, nothing. [long pause] So, that weekend kind of sucked, huh?

Monica: Yeah, it did.

Chandler: So, I guess this is over.

Monica: What?

Chandler: You and me? I guess it had to end sometime.

Monica: Why, exactly?

Chandler: Because of the weekend. We had a fight.

Monica: Chandler, that's crazy. If you give up every time you had a fight with someone, you'd never be with anyone longer than ... OHHHHH!!!

Chandler: So, this isn't over?

Monica: You are so cute. Oh, no. It was a fight. You deal with it and you move on. It's nothing to freak out about.

Chandler: Really? Okay, great.

Monica: Welcome to an adult relationship.

Chandler: We're in a relationship?

Monica: I'm afraid so.

Chandler: Okay.

I loved this episode. Not because of the fighting, obviously, but maybe because I have lived that conversation. Laugh if you must, but I guarantee I'm not the only person who sees "red flags" and starts to check out. I'm not a jealous person at all, but when things start to look "too difficult," I start to "reconsider." I mean, who has time to invest in something that isn't going anywhere, right? And, if our relationship is on suicide watch this early in the game, why bother investing time I don't have. (Can I get an amen?)

Sadly, perhaps, I've lived by this principle. Or maybe *fortunately*.

You get it. Or at least some of you do. I'm free for drinks most nights, so HMU (very cool millennial text talk right there).

Fights are never fun. And, as if I must write this, there is never a good time to have one. But I'm also going to help by adding that they are necessary. As my father always used to say, "If we agree on everything, one of us isn't necessary." It's healthy to disagree on things. That's called debate (or "collaboration" if you're too delicate for the word "debate").

So, the trick, I'm convinced, is not to avoid the fights, but to take some proactive measures to always ensure that *you* always win. (I'm kidding, of course, but if you didn't laugh at that, you need help.)

(You just went back and reread that sentence, didn't you?)

Really, though, there is a trick to the fighting – even at home. And the trick, is not trying to prove a point. Rather, I would argue, the trick is finding the "North Star." Spend your time looking for the reason it worked before. Keep the focus on the parts that *aren't* broken.

Now, insert the meme which schooled me.

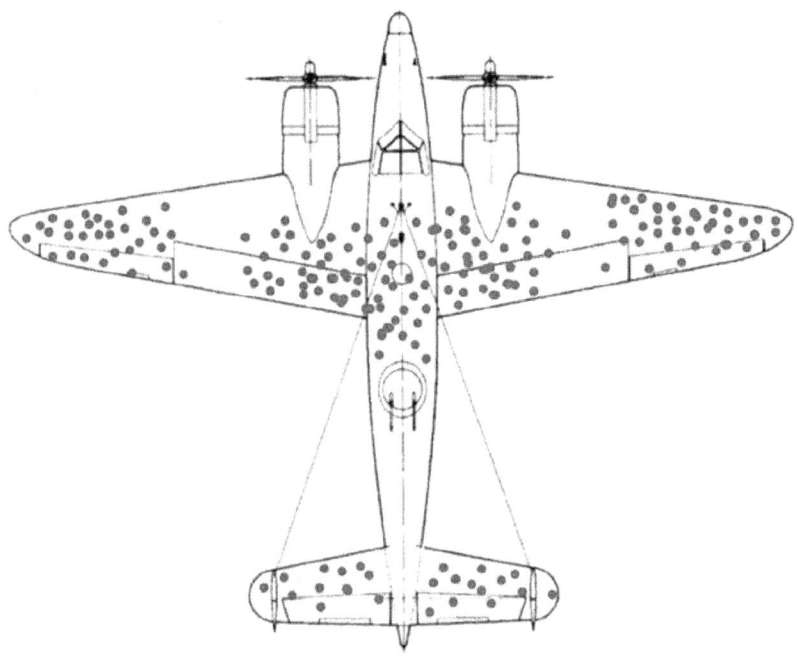

Seems like a strange image to get "schooled" by, but it was the caption which taught me the lesson. Beneath this photograph was a short story. It read something like this:

"During WWII, the navy was commissioned to determine where they needed to armor their aircraft to ensure that they came back home. After extensive research, resulting in the image above, they ran an analysis of where planes had been shot up, and concluded that the places that needed to be "up-armored" were the wingtips, the central

body, and the elevators. That's where the planes were all getting shot up, after all.

"Only one man, Abraham Wald, a statistician, disagreed. He thought they should better armor the nose area, the engines, and the mid-body. It sounded crazy, as those were not the areas the aircraft were even being hit. The difference, Mr. Wald realized, was something so obvious that the others had overlooked it entirely.

"The data was skewed, he explained. The only data the researchers had were the planes which survived the fire and made it home safely. He argued that, in fact, the aircraft which survived were likely the inverse of the planes which did not. Thus, they should reinforce the areas which kept the planes in the air. The planes which returned were able to survive the damage they had received, thus making those impacted areas less critical to survival. What the researchers had inadvertently done was analyze where the aircraft could suffer the most damage without catastrophic failure."

This was my a-ha moment.

Flashbacks of past "damage control" may have triggered some overly-symptomatic PTSD, but I suppose it's better late than never. How many times had I focused on repairing the damaged areas, rather than strengthening the areas which could have kept us airborne? I mean, why does it always seem so easy to find the differences but finding the "glue" is like nailing Jell-O to a tree. (If you have never tried nailing Jell-O to a tree, please put this book down and give it a whirl. It's a missed metaphor if you don't try. Send pics.)

I contend that we are conditioned to see differences. We are natural discriminators. We never see people like ourselves and think, "look how similar we are." Why? Because we expect it. We take similarity for granted, I'm afraid. If I see a woman at the mall dressed in traditional Indian garb, I notice it. It stands out. Not so much for the white guy in jeans and a t-shirt. Same with accents. Same with unusual hairdos. Same with political affiliations. I'd argue that we like living in our own little echo chambers - and it is natural. (I remember being on a trip to China once and learned this lesson the hard way. Let's say that the 6'4" white guy was a bit of a spectacle.)

Now comes the fun part: embracing diversity. Not always easy, I'll agree, but well worth the challenge. And, if you're still not convinced that we're predispositioned (if not conditioned) to find differences, watch the news.

Relationships are no different. Typically, people look for partners – even friends – with whom they have similarities, albeit common interests and goals. It's natural. It's healthy. We simply don't have the bandwidth to be constantly in disagreement with the people closest to us. We prefer to spend our time around people with whom we can relax and be ourselves.

Yet, conflict arises.

In romantic relationships, these differences tend to seem overwhelming at times, as we really don't get a lot of time away from our *one and only*. We are forced to deal with it. But do we deal with it effectively?

Imagine the case that every time a disagreement arose, both you and your partner were forced to pause the conversation and identify three ways in which your relationship is *not* broken.

You're mad because I didn't clean the house as I promised, but ...

1. I do work hard and always make sure the bills are paid.
2. I love the kids more than you ever imagined your spouse could.
3. I planned the best birthday party for you last month and you were so surprised.

Maybe I'm not so bad after all.

And just like with relationships, romantic or otherwise, business relationships need the same kind of nurturing.

Disagreements with clients are just as inevitable. They're not happy with the way your team handled a project or answered a phone call, but the isolated incident seems less of a problem when we stop and think through the ways in which things *did* go well.

Even in the business world, there is a kneejerk reaction to "throw out the baby with the bathwater." The minute there is a problem, clients tend to see it as being the new norm. Their dissatisfaction tends to be a focal point. And your response tends to be a defense. Let the games begin.

In our business, our work is constantly under scrutiny. It is marketing and things change, campaigns wane, and consumers are unpredictable. All clients want everything done within 24 hours. They want guaranteed ROI. And they want it done *pro bono*. (Sorry, clients, but I'm a client too. I'm just not *your* client.)

We're no exception. Our clients call us with concerns. They want changes. They don't love all our work (as most of it is subjective, until we have sufficient data to prove its efficacy, one opinion is no better than another, I guess). But, when they call, I always take the time to review the parts they *do* like.

In a recent website project, our team received a list of changes which would choke a horse. To the artist, it was a punch in the gut, honestly. It was a bulleted list of all the things the client disliked about his work. In usual fashion, I requested a phone call (face-to-face is better than voice-to-voice, but voice-to-voice beats email every time).

Being defensive of my team's work (it was really good work, actually), I began the meeting with the usual pleasantries, then asked them to start from the top of the home page and walk me through it, piece by piece (not the top of their bulleted list). As expected, they *loved* and gushed about 90+% of the work. In fact, once they were forced to comment on the many things they *loved* about the work, they removed several of the items from their list. They talked themselves out of the changes when they were forced to dialogue (not just craft an email).

If I may say, after that Zoom call, I felt our relationship was stronger than before. Three reasons:

1. They had to verbalize the things they *liked*.
2. They had to *justify* the things they didn't like.
3. They had to listen to the *reasons* behind the things they didn't like, which made them respect the work more and caused them to change their mind on several items.

It wasn't terribly complicated, but it was intentional. Rather than getting caught up in the drama of rejection, we spun it into a positive and produced better work. We spent our time focusing on the strengths, and not the weaknesses.

Like that WWII meme, we reinforced the areas which helped the mission succeed – and we landed the plane. To focus on the areas which appeared to most damaged would have left the other parts still vulnerable.

Double down on your strengths. Talk about them. Brag about them. Hell, write it down in a book and tell the world about them. But never, and I mean *never* forget them. The strengths are what keeps you together.

(And, if I'm being honest, the client had some good input. Funny how collaboration makes things better.)

Personal Confession

I've said it before: I'm a master debater. It's hereditary, I think, because my father is the same way. Master debating just seems to run in my family.

The truth is, I enjoy it. It's fun – but only if you're me, I guess. And once I start, people just don't want to engage. I end up sitting there by myself wondering why people get so caught up in their emotions. Was it something I said?

Debate, for me, is like a love language (take notes, Gary Chapman). It's an intellectual turn on. Make a solid case, then support it with reasons for your position (even if your support is an emotional response). Explain yourself – through facts or through experience.

As I have written previously, the goal of debate is to understand the opposing view and to make yourself equally understood. But what is often ignored in argument is that *emotional reactions* are relevant data. Personal experience is valid input and should always be validated.

Personally, I tend to get very robotic during an argument. My stoic approach to disagreement tends to be a real turnoff. I can be perceived as being detached - or even condescending (that means that people "think I am talking down to them").

Now, my go-to strategy is to always let the other person express their position first. I have learned that if I go first, the other person feels as if I have become disinterested or have tuned out.

Try it sometime.

From the CEO's Desk

You're going to find this quite hard to believe, but I find myself in the strangest situations. I mean, like Twilight Zone, Bizarro World stuff (please don't guess my age from those references). And, for whatever reason, I'm nearly almost the arbitrator. I mean, I like peace as much as the next guy, but constantly helping other people solve their problems? I have enough of my own.

Well, on one such occasion, I got stuck on a telephone call with this husband-and-wife business team. They owned a nail polish business in Arizona and were in a somewhat intense argument with a mutual contact to whom they owned money. Because of this dispute, the mutual contact decided to pull out of a deal in which we were *all* involved, so this did, indirectly, affect me. (I mean, they decided to just not pay him after he provided the services, so I understood his position. The trick in this mediation was to get them to understand and honor their commitments.)

The situation in more detail: He had introduced them to several people in the distribution world, but at a cost. What they did with the introductions, of course, was their responsibility. His fee was merely a percentage of whatever happened with his contacts (quite common). After the introductions, however, they felt that he "had not earned" the money and refused to pay (turns out this is habitual behavior for them, but I didn't know that at the time).

My goal in the conversation was to get them to see the value he had provided and to realize that they were losing a great relationship over a ridiculously small amount of money. They were burning bridges for no reason, and eventually, costing themselves a lot of heartache.

Practicing what I preach, I began focusing on the strengths of the relationships. What things *did* go as you planned? What is the value in *that*? Did they benefit from the introductions? To what degree did he play a role in that?

My goal was to reinforce the areas that kept the relationship afloat before. What helped that plane land in the past? Focusing on the strengths of the relationship, I was able to minimize the weaknesses and get this back on track.

They understood the point and were grateful for the sounding board. They did agree to pay the money they owed, and we moved forward with our other arrangement, although cautiously.

You see, fights are both opportunities to strengthen a relationship *and* to learn a lot about the quality of the opponent. In this instance, the fight, albeit resolved, showed the character of these people.

(Granted, this couple were also swingers and tried to get us to join their network, so I should have realized something was a bit strange then, but I'm not always the brightest.)

Ryze-ing to the Occasion

In a business where hating scrutiny is coded into our DNA, it is important that we prepare ourselves for criticism. Artists, by their very nature, are protective of their craft, so defensiveness is natural. And, in fairness, few clients stop to ask *why* something was done – implying that there was no thought behind the design.

To buffer the unwelcome news, we use three specific strategies, which are applicable to personal *and* professional scenarios, I would argue:

1. **Be present.** Conversations which may trigger emotional responses should never be had over email / text message. If a client is providing feedback, we insist that it is always delivered in person (voice-to-voice at a minimum). Screen shares and Zoom calls are better than telephone calls. Emails are great to outline bullet points but should only be used for reference.

2. **Allow for diversity of thought.** Typically, when our team is working on a project for a client, we try to provide several different options (such as with logo design). Not only does this allow for various points of view, but it also stops the artist from getting too attached to a single design. Usually, after conversation, we end up combining a couple of different designs into one – and it is always better because of the conversation.

3. **Neutral party mediation.** In all conversations we have with a client, there is an account manager hosting the meeting. Whether the conversation turns out to be a love fest, or a blood bath, someone is always present who can remain neutral and memorialize moments of agreement, while orchestrating compromise.

Using these tactics has led to incredibly effective conversations with our clients. And, I would argue, these same tactics can be used when navigating relationships.

Today's Lessons Learned

- In moments of crisis, focus on reinforcing your strengths and not your weaknesses.
- In relationships, there will always be conflict. Overcoming that conflict will require doubling down on the relationship's strengths.
- Expecting that conflict will occur, prepare for it and plan how you will overcome.
- Seeing differences is natural, but seeing similarities takes discipline.

Now, Ask Yourself

- Self, when conflict arises, how do you avert your attention from the negative and focus on the positive?
- Self, when conflict arises, where does your mind naturally go? How do you harness it?
- Self, what was the last time that you were successful in overcoming conflict? What worked?
- Self, have you identified any triggers that cause you to react emotionally in conflict situations? What can you do to control these?

On ignoring negativity.

CHAPTER 14: THE WALK OF SHAME

Repeat after me:

"*Alexa, play* Walkashame, *by Meghan Trainor."*

This should put you in the mood to accept the mess that's about to unfold in this chapter. It's like a custom playlist, really. Well, one song anyway.

While I'm not asking you to make a public confession about your most indulgent days in the dorms, let's talk through the college years a bit.

It's 7:00am.

Daylight is starting to pierce through the window shades. Your eyes slowly open and you are met with a regretful reality: This isn't your bed.

Eyes suddenly jarred open by the adrenaline-infused reality that you have no memories of the night before, you take a cautious inventory of your surroundings and recognize nothing.

Why is this so surreal? This can't be right.

It feels like a bad dream, but you're starting to piece together the events which have led to the cognitive failure you are now calling "morning." And, as you glance to your side, looking both left and right, you realize that things could have been worse. You flop back down and recreate the evening in your spinning head, only focusing on one thing: *How the hell do you get back to your own place without running into anyone you know?*

Folks make light of the "walk of shame" as being an embarrassing, bad hookup, but, if you'll indulge me a little here, I will argue that most of you had fun the night before. It was the *other people* in your life that made it feel so shameful. The shame came from the judgment; it wasn't the regret.

Amiright? (I did it again. You can check the dictionary.)

We've all made similar mistakes. In fact, I'd argue to say that you may not even remember all their names. You know who does though? Your friends!

It sucks, really, because you got into this with the hopes of having no emotional connection, and here you are dealing with emotion (or judgment, as it were).

The "walk of shame," in my generation, conjures images of some stray girl stumbling home after a night of ill-contemplated mischief. Shoes in hand and hair unkempt, she embarrassingly makes her way back to her dorm room, crushed by the judgment and jeers of her peers.

That said, however, I suffer from an insatiable curiosity for nonsense trivia and I couldn't continue this chapter without looking up the history of that phrase. The more vogue among you may only know the reference from your irreverent days in college, but you would be surprised to learn that it didn't get its first mention in that context until the early nineties.

According to my stealth-like research, the phrase experienced its first usage in the military, where it was said to be used to describe a soldier who "tapped out" during training exercises. (Sounds a bit less trivial than your barefoot parade through campus with strappy heals wrapped around your wrists.) In military terms, it was a devastating event. I mean, a poorly-judged one-night stand is not the same as committing professional suicide.

Taking the "walk of shame" in the military is considered the ultimate failure for a bootcamp enrollee. Picture a young cadet, perhaps following in his father's footsteps and joining the proud and the strong. He suffers unbearable training throughout his tenure in bootcamp, but on a day that feels more unbearable than the others, he quits. He throws in the towel. He decides that this path just is too much and yields to the discomfort.

Emotionally burdened by visions of his future (sharing his failure with his family, thinking of alternative career choices, and some personal defeat), he now must walk past each of his peers who have the resolve to endure.

His "walk of shame" is a public spectacle. He didn't get to pack his things in the middle of the night and leave quietly. In fact, part of his punishment was to parade his failure in full sight of those who did not succumb to the same temptation. (If you're a Game of Thrones fan, liken this to Cersei's parade through Kings' Landing. It's like that, but not naked.)

That visual is much more powerful than a stroll back to the dormitory, but both could be devastating to a person's self-worth.

Think it's a stretch to make the comparison between a bad hookup and a business deal? Indulge me.

Anyone who has spent as much as six minutes in sales understands the excitement of a *laydown*. It's the contract that got signed so easily that your self-esteem grew three sizes that day. You started to believe your own press releases and may have even told everyone about how easy this was – *or maybe you're just that good.*

I mean, life would be great if we didn't have to get too invested in things and we could still feel good about it.

Then the inevitable happens. The client turns into your worst nightmare. Sure, the contract is signed, but, for whatever reason, it is a yeoman's task to keep these people satisfied. Non-stop questions. Complaints. Incessant asks for adjustments to policies. It's as if they never read the contract before they signed it! Wait, what?! That happens?

It's that good time that just keeps coming back to haunt you, and worse than that sorority strut, everyone in the office sees it happening. The party just turned into a hangover.

We've all had it happen. No matter how hard you try to avoid it, some deals just slip past our better judgment and get the best of us. Perhaps it just looks too tempting to pass up. Or perhaps you were just in a dry spell, so you were willing to sign anything. Regardless, the deed is done and now you're left dealing with the consequences – praying they end soon and swearing you learned your lesson.

You may be surprised to learn that failure is common. In fact, I'd argue that we've all had our turn. I'd even wager that I've had more than you. (You know how to reach me if you'd like to take that dare.)

And, although you may be frequently reminded of your failures by those who know you best, I'm going to offer some advice on dealing with these misfortunes.

1. **Don't take it personally.** One of the gravest mistakes a person can make is not learning how to separate failure from identity. Failure is an event; it is not a person. When a failure happens, own it, but don't move in. Some of the greatest people in history had a past laced with failures.

Look at Abraham Lincoln. He failed in business at age 21; was defeated in a legislative race at age 22; failed again in business at 24; overcame the death of his fiancée at 26; had a nervous breakdown at 27; lost a congressional race at 34; lost a senatorial race at age 45; failed to become Vice President at age 47; lost a senatorial race at 49; and was elected as the President of the United States at the age of 52. He refused to let his failures define him and fought against significant odds to achieve greatness. Be like Abe.

2. **Learn and adapt.** Regardless of the nature of your plunge, there is always a cause – a root *something* that triggered your decision. Was it loneliness? Fear? Blind optimism? You better figure it out, sister, because you now need to find ways to safeguard against letting it happen again. Be objective and learn from it.

    Thomas Edison reportedly failed 10,000 times while he was inventing the light bulb. He was quoted as saying, "I have found 10,000 ways something won't work. I am not discouraged, because every wrong attempt discarded is another step forward." The Wright brothers spent years working on failed aircraft prototypes and incorporating their learnings until they finally got it right: a plane that could get airborne and stay there. Be like Orville and Wilbur.

3. **Stop dwelling on it.** This is a strange lesson served up by Captain Obsess-much, but one that has been learned the hard way. It's normal to give yourself some time to deal with the guilt / shame / regret of a setback, but set a limit. My rule is one day. Everyone in my life knows that if I'm in a "funk," leave me alone for exactly one day and I'll come back fighting.

    Don Shula is the winningest coach in the NFL, holding the record for most career wins (including two Super Bowl victories) and the only perfect season in NFL history.

Shula had a "24-hour rule," a policy of looking forward instead of dwelling on the past. The coach allowed himself, his staff and his players 24 hours to celebrate a victory or brood over a defeat. During those 24 hours, Shula encouraged them to feel their emotions of success or failure as deeply as they could. The next day, it was time to put it behind them and focus their energy on preparing for their next challenge. His philosophy was that if you keep your failures and victories in perspective, you'll do better in the long run.

4. **Release the need to please others.** As a senior member of People Pleasers Anonymous (although I guess my cover is blown now), I beg you to stop worrying about the opinions of others. In fact, I will let you in on a secret here: You spend more time thinking about what other people are thinking of you than all other people actual spend thinking of you – collectively. Let it go.

   Oprah Winfrey was fired from her first TV job because someone thought she was "unfit for TV." Stephen King's first book, Carrie, was rejected by 30 publishers. Walt Disney was fired from his newspaper job because he "lacked imagination and innovative ideas." Winston Churchill failed sixth grade and was considered "a dolt" by his teacher. Jerry Seinfeld was booed off the stage the first time he tried comedy. Soichiro Honda was rejected by an HR manager at Toyota Motor Corporation when he applied for an engineering job, leaving him jobless until he began making scooters in his garage and eventually founded Honda Motor Company. 'Nuff said. (Although, I may have fired Oprah too.)

5. **Try a new point of view.** I remember a conversation with my father one day when I was young. I was asking how he could pick up the telephone and cold call the way he did. For me, I explained, it would just be too much rejection. He said

to me, "Statistically, I have a one in ten shot at getting a 'yes' from a client. Each time I get a 'no,' I'm just one call closer to my deal." Maybe blind optimism, but that's called *flipping the script*.

Michael Jordan said it best: "I have missed more than 9,000 shots in my career. I have lost almost 300 games. On 26 occasions I have been entrusted to take the game-winning shot, and I missed. I have failed over and over and over again in my life. And that is why I succeed."[i]

Personal defeats, and professional alike, hurt. They trigger a range of emotions, but regardless of the circumstances, they are temporary. Life has a way of taking our weakest moments and holding us hostage with them, I understand, but what often feels like a crippling blow will pass; I promise.

Can I let you in on a secret? I love movies. The movies that move me most though are those in which the hero overcomes some terrible adversity or setback. Like Neo in the *Matrix*. Or Maximus in the *Gladiator*. They're *becoming* something throughout the story – and they overcome. They're our heroes.

And guess who is the hero of *your* story? Your failures can set the stage for an incredible comeback. Take a minute. Learn from it. Then get back up and strut it out.

"*Alexa, play* I Will Survive *by Gloria Gaynor.*"

: : : :

: : : :

: : : :

: : : :

"Alexa, now play The World's Greatest *by R. Kelly."*

(Don't you *dare* judge me. That song fires me up.)

Personal Confession

It took me a lot of years to be okay with failure (as much as anyone can be okay with failure). I mean, who is ever okay with failure? But, over time, I realized that each time I felt as if *it was over*, I got back up and managed to rise stronger and better than the time before. Much like a pruning, for the gardeners among us.

Failure, and that walk of shame, feels gross. Often, it messes with our sense of self-worth. It creates hauntings of doubt that become *literally* crippling. Funny enough, that's never been my problem. I have always been able to psych myself into getting back on the horse and trying again. The one thing that kept me on the ground was the shame of public opinion.

If I fail, everyone will see.

I was less afraid of the failure than I was of the spectacle I was convinced it was going to create. When I realized that this was my handicap though (my "junk," as my therapist put it), it is as if the world opened up to me. Realizing that the opinions of others had no impact on me, I became liberated to try any number of new things without any fear.

All successes are built from a series of failures. Every. Single. One. Embracing the failures allows us a chance to study for the future. I think of coach making the team watch video of their last game. He doesn't do it to torture them with their failure; he does it to highlight the ways in which their game could improve. Periodically, I play my highlight reel in my head: *Mark's Greatest Failures*. Sometimes I cringe. Sometimes I laugh. Sometimes I don't even recognize the guy in that playback. Those milestone failures have provided so much feedback. It has been my own bootcamp experience, and I have done my own "walk of shame" multiple times.

Failing is human. What you do with it is what sets you apart.

From the CEO's Desk

I'm not exaggerating when I tell you that I often spend my days feeling like a counselor. I get the chance to spend time with so many business owners and aspiring entrepreneurs, each with their own story of interwoven successes and failures. The background stories are so predictable and usually begin with a phrase like "our plan was to ..." or "what we meant to do was ..."

We all get it. Things didn't go as planned. They seldom do, dear heart, and that puts you in the majority – *not the minority*. Your business ... your marriage ... your financial plan ... whatever it is, it didn't go as planned. It could be for any number of reasons, but you're not so unique. It makes me smile when people disclose their shame from a recent failure. I smile thinking, "Good. You're ready to make a change."

My favorite clients are those which have experienced doing it the *wrong way*. They already know they don't know everything. They're eager for help. They are willing to talk about contingency plans because they know that it doesn't always go as planned. They've *matured*.

Ryze-ing to the Occasion

More often than you would believe, we receive client requests from businesses seeking marketing services. They know exactly what they want. Sometimes, they are so certain about what they want that I wonder if they need marketing services at all. And my favorite stipulation is when they let us know that they will pay us "per sale." [imagine my face twisting a little as I scratch my chin]

They are willing to allow us to spend our own time and money to sell their product, but then suggest that they only pay us if something sells.

While I have no interest in that kind of arrangement (nor does anyone else, so I'll save you the hassle of making those calls), it always sounds like a person who is afraid to fail. They are so certain in the future success of the strategies they brought to us, *they are willing to let us take the risk.* I mean, it sounds like a great setup if they find someone willing to play along, but it is unlikely.

We bet on ourselves every day. We bet our own reputation that we can move the needle for our clients' businesses (as well as our own internally-owned brands). We bet that our clients will have no reason to talk ugly about us. And the bet seems to work. Arguably 100% of our client base is a referral from someone else in our network.

We believe that we do work so well that people will want to tell their friends. Bank on it.

Today's Lessons Learned

- Don't take failure personally. It describes an event, but not a person.
- The only mistakes that are losses are the ones you don't learn from.
- Most shame associated with a failure is only related to public opinion. Shake it off.
- The greatest stories ever told are about a hero who overcomes a great challenge. Be the hero of your story.

Now, Ask Yourself

- Self, when you find yourself defeated be a setback, what is the thing you fear most? Is it related to the opinion of others?
- Self, when you experience these setbacks, how can you frame them as learning opportunities, rather than failures?
- Self, when was the last time that you made an error in judgment that stressed you this way? How did you cope and how could you have coped better?
- Self, who are the people you trust enough to speak truth to you when your confidence is faltering? Have you devised a system of accountability with them to avoid future setbacks?

On maintaining dignity.

Chapter 15: The Breakup

Like it or not, breakups happen.

And, while that two-word phrase does little to console the spirit of the rebuffed, it's about as accurate as it gets (#realtalk). I mean, really. We've all been through a breakup at some point. Sometimes it is cause for some cheering and a few drinks, admittedly, but, overall, breakups are the worst.

Recently, I was reading some trash magazines ... er ... I mean, "educational journals," and read a few articles that attempted to break down the breakup. I've compiled my own list; consider it a concatenated paraphrase of the "Truths About Breakups."

Here. I'll share them with you, and you can decide for yourself if it is "scream-worthy."

1. **Breaking up is always a hard decision.** I mean, unless you're a country singer, nobody wins in a breakup. Even the deciding partner goes through great stress, turmoil, and vodka making that kind of decision. The truth is, change is hard, and making the decision to finally rip off that bandage can be a grueling struggle. All the what-ifs and if-he-would-only thoughts argue against it – night and day.

2. **It's gonna suck – a lot.** Even the necessary breakups (you know the ones) are going to hurt. Regardless of the length of the relationship, there is a feeling of loss. The loss, in some instances, may be the person, the memories, or the

companionship; but I think one of the biggest losses for most people is the regret of the time they now see as "wasted." Months, years, or even decades can be spent poorly invested.

3. **You will lose friends.** I hate to break it to you, pumpkin, but you will lose people. Mutual friends no longer see you guys as a team, so they gravitate to the individual who is most valuable (or most convenient). It's normal. It's not an indictment on either of you, really. Sometimes, mutual friends drop you both, because they don't want to be put in the position of choosing (cowards!).

4. **Loneliness is not optional.** Even if you're the king or queen of the rebound game, after a breakup, things are not the same. Beds are bigger with only one person in them. Loss is loss. And even the loss of a mistake is still a loss. It's healthy to "embrace the suck" and heal. Make it a learning moment. Remember, sugar, everyone has an @sshole; you just had two.

5. **Things get better.** Statistically, I would be willing to put money on two things right now: 1) you have been through a breakup, and 2) you're still alive. (I mean, if you're not alive, shouldn't you be out voting or something?) Really, though, humans are resilient, above all things. We adapt. We change. We get even (just kidding ... kinda). But we heal. We find new ways to have value and new people to find value in us.

It's not a fun topic, of course, but a necessary one. Dating, after all, is a risk.

I once said to a friend that I hated dating because there were other things I would rather do with my time than waste it on someone who was not going to be in my life long-term anyway. I could be putting in my 10,000 hours into some new conquest. And, while I would still argue that case: nothing ventured, nothing gained. It's a gamble when you bet on people, and learning to cut bait is the best lesson available.

My best advice on the topic:

1. **Make intellectual, and not emotional, decisions.** The heart is deceptive.

2. **Plan your next moves in advance.** Even before the breakup, decide (proactively) what you're going to do in place of this relationship. Honestly, it makes the loneliness keep to a minimum. Find a hobby or something; fill that void with something intentional (or other things creep in).

Breakups aren't just for lovers though. Some of the most painful breakups I have ever had in my life have been professional. I mean, let's face it: I spend more time with the folks at the office than I do anyone outside of the office. They're just as much a part of my life as anyone in my family or friends' circle. A fight, a fallout, or even a loss of one of them hurts just as bad.

And for the entrepreneurs out there, maybe you have been where I have been before and lost your entire business. (To someone who has never walked in those shoes – you have no idea.) I can only liken it to a long-term marriage ending in an abrupt divorce. Suddenly, you're thrust into this identity crisis that nobody can solve. There is a feeling of "why don't people want me?" and "but, I did everything I could" that cannot be shaken. So many questions.

The defeat can be devastating, to say the least. And this can be equally true of losing a large client or project, as those losses can easily lead to the loss of the business entirely – or even your career.

Put on your big girl panties here because things are about to get real. I'm going to give you some of the scariest entrepreneurial statistics you've ever read. Did you know that,

- The number one reason that most businesses fail is because there is simply no market demand for their product / service?

- Approximately 80% of small businesses fail in less than 18 months?

- About two-thirds of small business owners use personal funds to deal with financial trouble in a business?

- Over two-thirds of small businesses carry outstanding debt?

- Only half of entrepreneurs report that they make more money being self-employed than when they were in the traditional workforce?

- None of these statistics matter to an entrepreneur, because entrepreneurs, by our very nature, attempt to defy the odds? (And, for the record, none of these numbers matter anyway, because everyone has a variation on the same statistic and measures it differently.)

Then why go through the semantics of listing all these numbers? Well, because if you're one of the crazy ones (like me), these numbers just give you a rule to break. If most businesses go out of business in a year, *watch me prove them wrong*. If most businesses go out of business in two years, *watch me prove them wrong*. If most businesses go out of business in five years, *watch me prove them wrong too*.

We're crazy. We're the hopeless romantics of the business world who keep falling in love over and over and over again, because we just know that *it will eventually work*.

Do you want to know when the numbers matter most? Read these.

- Approximately 62% of billionaires are self-made.

- In 2016, 25-million Americans ran their own businesses.

- About 60% of all small businesses are started by people over the age of 40.

- There are roughly 582-million entrepreneurs in the world.

- Just over 33% of all entrepreneurs have anything more than a high school diploma.

- Exactly 83.1% of all US business owners started their own companies (and still own them).

- Only 9% of business owners hold a bachelor's degree in business.

And, most importantly:

- *Of all self-employed professionals surveyed, 97% of them said that they would never go back to traditional employment.*

There it is. Exactly the point. A business owner is no more going to stop being a business owner than a hopeless romantic is going to stop looking for love. Sure, the game changes, and you learn along the way, but it is simply rooted in his/her DNA.

Now, let's go back to that list of "Truths About Breakups" and talk about some of those business failures (and how to cope).

1. **Breaking up is always a hard decision.** There is no business owner (or even manager) alive who has ever closed a business without significant bouts of insomnia. It is torture to make those kinds of decisions, including layoffs, branch closures, and even permanent closures. I've known a lot of people who have closed their businesses and I've rarely seen more tears shed.

2. **It's gonna suck – a lot.** Although most business cutbacks and closures are out of necessity, it doesn't make it any easier to deal with it. You're jobless, after all. You're trying to deal with the "could-a, should-a, would-a" scenarios of how you made mistakes. You'll place blame. You'll accept blame. You'll graffiti the walls with it, but it doesn't change the outcome. It ended. Learn from it and know it wasn't time wasted.

3. **You will lose friends.** People will leave you, so you know. Sometimes they are vendors who you thought were friends, but they only benefited from your business. Sometimes "loyal" employees are suddenly not loyal when the paychecks end. Sometimes even friends and family members become scarce when the going gets rough. You're of no benefit anymore.

4. **Loneliness is not optional.** At the end of the game, all the pieces end up back in the box, right? And all those people who were "in it with you" went and found other jobs. Sadly, it is *your* savings that is gone. It is *your* 401(k) that got cashed in. It is *your* credit that took a hit. Everyone else loves playing the game with you. And they love the enthusiasm that you rally. But, ultimately, you're in this alone.

5. **Things get better.** Every single failure is an opportunity to learn. Oh, it hurts so much, but I have never been in a painful situation that didn't teach me something and prepare me for the next adventure on the horizon (usually one I didn't even plan for). Learn. Learn so much. And when you're all done crying, even if it's over a bankruptcy, you put your big girl panties back on, and you do it again (Lots of big girl panties in this chapter. Weird.)

Nobody ever said it would be easy, but let's go back to the best advice you ever received (in this chapter, of course).

My best advice on the topic:

1. **Make intellectual, and not emotional, decisions.** The heart is deceptive.

2. **Plan your next moves in advance.** Even before the closure/loss/layoff, decide (proactively) what you're going to do next. Do nothing without purpose. And remember that every new beginning comes from some other beginning's end. (Deep thoughts sponsored by Semisonic: "Closing Time.")

PERSONAL CONFESSION

I have so many stories to tell here, but I'll keep it to a minimum (don't want to make you my therapist, after all). The truth is, however, I am guilty of mixing personal and business relationships. Being a person who always thinks the best of people (believe it or not), I frequently confuse people's interest in a job with their loyalty to me.

Quite recently, I had a staff person who I mistook for a close friend. For real, it felt like he was just a younger version of me – in so many ways. I invested and invested in his success, both with sharing my time and experience, as well as sharing my finances freely. I treated him like a partner in a lot of my investments. I paid for vacations, cars, and even made him a shareholder in a few of my businesses. You can only imagine my confusion when one day I received an email that he was considering leaving the company and moving out of state. An email. Yes. An email.

The reasons aside, although I found them to be suspect, I was even more confused when I learned that he lied about most of it and had accepted a position elsewhere. I was shocked. I was hurt. I was scared, honestly, as I had allowed him to take on such a leadership role in my company that I wasn't sure how to divorce him from it. I began my five steps.

Step One: Cutting ties was hard, but it had to be done. And done swiftly.

Step Two: I spent way too much time rehearsing what I could have done differently. I questioned all my actions, wondering if I did something to cause this, often assuming blame.

Step Three: I lost a friend. I think that loss was worse than the business loss, but I couldn't explain why, because none of it made sense.

Step Four: I found myself working on a lot of projects alone now. I lost my collaborator: my sounding board.

Step Five: Things are so much better now. I mean, *so much better*. His leaving did two primary things for my business:

- It forced me to grab the steering wheel again, which is where I thrive. My team is stronger for it.

- It allowed other talent to bubble to the surface and take on leadership roles. We had more talent here in the building than I even realized, because someone else held it at bay.

What a gift!

If you wait long enough, you'll see how things are working in your favor. They always are. Shut up and quit crying long enough to see it.

Years prior, I had a similar experience with another employee. This one was the mother of a close friend of mine (well, ex-girlfriend, but we're still cool). She worked for me many years back doing payroll. She was great – so I thought. She was like a surrogate mom to me in a lot of ways (and I was like her *normal* child).

Anyway, business took a downturn after the loss of a large client. Again, the losses. We had to make some tough decisions about staffing at the time, but when I was talking to our operations manager, I *insisted* that the mom of my ex-girlfriend not be impacted. (Sorry, but I had to phrase it that way because it just makes that sentence funnier.) We worked on a plan and, although we didn't need a full-time payroll manager anymore (that was one of the cuts), we were going to move her to customer service and layoff someone on that team to accommodate.

I was so happy when I called her to let her know *personally* that the loss of revenue was not going to impact her job – albeit it was going to change the nature of the work.

Oh. My. Word. If you could have listened to that conversation.

I fast learned that the "I would do anything for you" ended at "we have to adjust your responsibilities." In a matter of 20 minutes, not only did I have an opening in customer service, I was blocked on social media, read the riot act about how she has sacrificed so much for the business, and was told that she was going to call the IRS on me (because she had files at her house that had social security numbers on them and it was my problem to get them out of her living room).

Thanks, mom.

From the CEO's Desk

I was a business owner back as far as 16 years old. Yes, it's true. I had to hire people to work at my business when I was in high school. So funny to look back at it now. I learned *everything* the hard way. I mean, *everything*. What I wouldn't have given for a mentor back then.

BUT, and that's a very big "but" (say that out loud and it is hilarious), but it forced me to learn all of the things in such a concentrated way that I was able to make a splash very early in life. But splashes often lead to drowning. Such is the case with me.

You can imagine my pain when at 23 years old, I found myself having to look for a real job. I mean, I had never had a real job before. I was a top performing retailer in our field, with multiple locations, when ... suddenly ... there was no market demand for our products anymore. (You'll recall that the number one reason that most businesses fail is because there is simply no market demand for their product / service?) I wasn't prepared. I didn't know how to be. I sold my business for a fraction of what it would have been worth just a year or two prior, then had to make a résumé.

Young, cocky, egotistical me had to go sell myself. It felt very prostitute-y.

You'll be happy to know that I got kicked in the teeth quite a few times. I certainly found employment quickly but learned that the world didn't bend to my whim. I had to budget and save and do other pedestrian things. And, if I can be honest, it took a toll on my self-worth. I blamed myself for the loss. I felt that the failure made *me* a failure more than it made the *business* a failure. And it took me years to realize that the business didn't "fail." It didn't fail any more than a person who breathes their last breath "fails." It just ended. It was time. But tell that to 23-year-old me, however, and I wouldn't have heard it. My identity was shaken. Badly.

You know what it did though? It made me the best damn employee anyone else would ever have. I knew so many things that my career skyrocketed. Fast. I learned and didn't even know I was learning.

And here I am. I am writing prose to tickle your eyeballs, talking about the events that I would have sworn would be my demise.

Things get better.

Ryze-ing to the Occasion

Being the eternal optimist certainly has its share of risks. Primarily, I struggle to end relationships before the devolve into a septic mess.

Sometimes they're employees who need to leave. Other times, they're clients who have overstayed their welcome.

While I am always humane in my decisions and value relationships over transactions, I have learned the art of being pragmatic in my philanthropy. I have had to terminate more than my fair share of staff people throughout my career but have never lost the empathy for the other person's loss. Several times, I have found myself talking to a staff person about the need for a breakup, but then spend time discussing how I can help the person strategize a new gig. Heck, I've terminated people and then helped them get into rehab.

Our greatest intention is to recognize the value of the person – even if the person is not a good fit for our organization. People have value.

Today's Lessons Learned

- Although breakups are always hard, they are sometimes necessary. Be intentional.
- When deciding to end a relationship, either professional or personal, plan, as there are several considerations.
- Failure is merely a part of the journey. Learn from it.
- Failure is an event. It is not a person. Don't internalize.

Now, Ask Yourself

- Self, when was the last time that you had to decide to terminate a relationship? Is there something you would have done differently?
- Self, do you tend to internalize and accept full responsibility for things when they end? How do you stop taking that blame?
- Self, when faced with these types of decisions, do you act rationally, or do you get lost in your emotions?
- Self, how do you ensure that the other party is treated with value and dignity, regardless of the circumstances?

On growing too comfortable.

Chapter 16: Netflix and Chill

Too many hours of my life have already been lost to my love affair with Netflix. It's shameful to admit, honestly. I pride myself on being a focused, driven achiever-type, but I can hold a deep, meaningful conversation about nearly any binge-worthy show available on your favorite streaming service (unless it's something stupid like Downton Abbey … I said what I said).

It requires absolutely no effort on my part to lose myself in someone else's life for a while. Sometimes, I love the escape from my own stressful day, but other times, I can't even tell you why I turned it on. It has just become that much of a habit.

Here I am, work hard, play hard, man-on-the-move, in-the-gym-every-day-guy, and I'm confessing to binge-watching on Netflix. I mean, if you've already made it to chapter 16, I should be taking advice from you, I think, because you're the one holding a book. I'm probably sitting with a bowl of popcorn and a rerun of Dexter.

But indulge me for a moment here. While the phrase "Netflix and chill" may have some colloquial connotations, there is something to be said about the dangers of growing too comfortable.

In his book, *Good to Great*, author Jim Collins makes the following statement: "Good is the enemy of great." Collins arrested complacency. He calls out the lackluster of "good enough." And, while Collins discussed this concept in the context of business goals, there are greater applications to be made.

It's Friday night and she's gotten all excited about "date night" (because, after all, Friday night is date night, right?). She composes an excited text to ask what's on the agenda for the evening. A bit later, she receives the "What about Netflix and chill?" response.

A *night in* doesn't sound like a bad idea, but that's been the plan for the last three months. Same old, same old. No excitement. No adventure. Pizza and a movie on the couch. It lacks a certain romance, honestly, but what happened that has made this too-often-repeated itinerary acceptable. When did complacency replace the excitement of time together?

Well, I'll help here, because there are signs that things are growing too comfortable. Easy to detect, these barriers are just as easy to remove, but it takes time away from Netflix, I'll warn you.

- **Sign #1: You're always putting things off.** Perhaps you delay conversations or even prioritize time with others, you're not placing your relationship in a priority position. Insidious, I argue that this is the most dangerous of all the signs, as it leads to neglect. And neglect can kill the spirit.

    I've been the recipient of the "can I call you back" ghostings. I assure you that that nothing will crush someone like feeling deprioritized. I promise that the recipient of such a text is itemizing everything on which your time is spent and making this self-statement: "I am less important than _____."

- **Sign #2: You don't do the things you once enjoyed.** Hobbies and shared interests should build a relationship. They should form bonds and create shared experiences. Having your own hobbies and time alone is great, but having shared interests not only builds a shared community, but it also creates shared goals and makes shared memories.

Too often, couples pride themselves of having completely different hobbies, communities, and, honestly, different lives. Couples who spend too much time apart can start to create competing goals with their partner, and even begin building stronger relationships with other people. That's dangerous territory.

- **Sign #3: You take your partner for granted.** Perhaps the entire point of this chapter, your partner should always be a priority in your life. I remember a mentor of mine once making the statement: "I can learn everything I need to know about your priorities by merely looking at your calendar and your checkbook." Succinctly, where you spend your time and money is where you see the value.

Are you being intentional about time with your partner? Are you just settling for Netflix and chill? Would it really take too much more effort to cook dinner together prior to the movie night, if that's what you enjoy?

- **Sign #4: Sarcasm creeps in.** It's easy to get snarky when you're too comfortable. But even jokes can start to hurt when guards are down. Remember that your opinion should matter more to your partner than anyone in the world. What are you doing with your words?

Are your words uplifting and positive? Have your words grown calloused? If your partner needs to hear the words, "I love you," is it too much to indulge him/her? The ask clearly reveals a need. Protect that person with your words.

- **Sign #5: Sex is no longer sexy.** I can write nothing better than this quote by psychologist Piper Grant: "It is great when sex can be comfortable between two people, and they feel free to be themselves sexually, yet when sex becomes so routine and bland that each person literally takes off their own clothes, lays down and tries to be the first to say 'I call bottom,' then the comfort level has also become not so sexy."

Sex is the epitome of excitement in a committed relationship, and while excitement can ebb and flow, it can be used as a barometer of relational health. I contend that no amount of justifying your relationship's sexual heat will change the fact that you feel the need to justify it. I'll go on record as stating that no human alive doesn't want to have a satisfying sex life. But when it isn't, ask yourself why. Then, for f***'s sake, fix it. (Literally.)

- **Sign #6: You're not minding your manners.** It's easy to be casual around your one true love, but when things get too sloppy, fire up the inquisition. It's true that your partner should love you even at your worst, but if you quit caring what that person thinks of you, things may have gotten a little too comfortable.

  Above all humans on this blue marble, your partner's opinion should matter most. Sweatpants are great for sick days but get your lazy *ss off the couch occasionally and show her that you own an outfit worthy of at least a four-star experience. Also, fart jokes are never funny. Ever.

- **Sign #7: You're not fully engaged in conversations.** I read a meme recently which made this point perfectly. It read: "My wife started a fight with me out of nowhere the other day. I mean, who starts a conversation by yelling, 'Are you even listening to me?'"

  When you're disconnected, it is obvious. And it all gets back to the deprioritizing point. If you're not paying attention to me, what is more important? Put down the phone. Make eye contact. You may find the conversation is interesting.

- **Sign #8: You don't actively show appreciation.** This may be the most important item on this list. Did you know that gratitude increases happiness by a measurable 10%? And it reduces depressive symptoms by a measurable 35%? And it lasts!

    Showing your partner how much you appreciate the value he/she brings to your life not only has a positive impact on your own psyche, but it will also inspire the other person to do more things to make you grateful.

It may read like a laundry list of warning signs to help avoid a boring homelife, but this Netflix trap is real. I would argue that too many people pride themselves on being so comfortable with each other that they don't "have to" do anything but "chill" to be happy. I call BS on that.

I also call BS on the person who says that their clients are happy and loyal and require little maintenance. No client is on autopilot and treating them that way is a recipe for making them someone else's client. I promise. You are never going to ignore your way to a better relationship. They don't want to be "left alone." And when they tell you that they are good and don't need anything right now, there is a hidden meaning. I'm going to decode that for you: "I don't need anything right now but thank you for reminding me that you're available if something does arise."

Don't avoid weekly touch-base calls. Don't delay replying to the emails. Don't ignore the client paying the bills because you're busy landing the next big deal. Don't ignore the customer feedback surveys. And, for cripes' sake, don't believe that your best review is representative of your average customer's opinion.

Let's go back through those warning signs one more time and see if they apply to our professional lives as I predict.

- **Sign #1: You're always putting things off.** Guaranteed warning sign that things could go south if you're always delaying work and not hitting deadlines. Never make your client feel deprioritized.

- **Sign #2: You don't do the things you used to enjoy.** Your client needs to believe that their business is as important to you as it is to them. Do you collaborate anymore or are you just another vendor on retainer?

- **Sign #3: You take your partner for granted.** Have you started missing the weekly touch-base calls? Stopped sending the progress reports? Stopped communicating like you used it?

- **Sign #4: Sarcasm creeps in.** Are you so comfortable with your client that your language has even gone casual? Have you found yourself talking about them in a negative tone – even if it is only to your coworkers? That negativity starts to seep through cracks and invade our thoughts. And thoughts lead to behaviors.

- **Sign #5: Sex is no longer sexy.** Well, don't have sex with your clients (says the guy who is telling you to date them), but remember that there was once passion. You both were excited about working together. Where has that gone? *They want it back.*

- **Sign #6: You're not minding your manners.** Recently, I was copied on an email from a partner company (we have a mutual client). The spelling and grammar made my red pen run in terror. I thought to myself, "Do you realize you're sending the message to your client that they are not even important enough for you to spellcheck?"

- **Sign #7: You're not fully engaged in conversations.** Are you 100% present when you're talking to your client? I've been on plenty of Zoom calls lately and the amount of distraction going on in the background has given me shivers.

- Don't think they feel like they're your focus when you are writing other emails, answering phone calls, and shushing a barking dog during your strategy calls.

- **Sign #8: You don't actively show appreciation.** Aside from just providing good service at a fair price, do you take the time to tell your clients how much you personally appreciate working with them. Do they know that? Do they hear about it - outside of the annual Christmas card?

Whether personal or professional, this idea of getting too comfortable can have some abysmal consequences. The greatest cause of getting too comfortable: distraction.

In a busy, busy world, we move from priority to priority without a lot of regard for the corner stones. The relationships which put us on the map can be temporary if we don't consistently nurture them and intentionally make them *feel* like priority.

I'm using the feeling words there, you'll notice. It's not what you do that matters; it is how they feel about what you're doing. Know the difference. Autopilot is not a thing in the world of relationships.

PERSONAL CONFESSION
_____

Regretfully, we all have *Netflix and Chill* stories, I'm afraid. They sneak up and bite you sometimes, like snakes in the grass. But, if we're being honest, what seems like "suddenly" wasn't sudden at all.

I am certain that if you hold so much as a high school diploma you have heard the "tale of the boiling frog." According to urban myth, if you place a frog in a pot of boiling water, it will instantly leap out. In contrast, however, if you place a frog in a pot of pleasantly tepid water, then gradually heat the water, the frog will boil to death, lacking the ability to notice the minor changes in temperature. He learned how to adapt so well that it led to his death.

Easy lesson: Don't be the frog.

Harder lesson: Be watchfully vigilant the signs which lead to gradual decay in your relationships.

I remember a time when, back in my early twenties, this happened to me. Without a lot of details, I will say that I was in an incredible relationship when I was young (and stupid). I was so happy, and things were so easy. So easy.

Beautiful, smart, sassy, sexy ... she had it all. I was all in. She was perfect, I thought. In two years, we hadn't even had a real disagreement. In retrospect, we never learned how to "work at a relationship," because this just came so easily. Then, after two years of a great relationship, life got more complicated, and we were too immature to realize what was happening – or how to correct it.

Here I was, assuming that things were too good to end. I was a great boyfriend. I was stable. I was thoughtful. I loved her family and they loved me back. We were financially doing well and were on a professional rise. It was happening.

She felt the same way. We were happy in love and things were great. But when things started getting too comfortable, we began to neglect "us." Career. Family. Personal commitments. Living arrangements. They all started to steal our time together, and in the moments we were able to share, we got lazy about prioritizing each other.

I remember that first fight. I don't remember what it was about, but I remember the argument – even where I was sitting when it happened. I remember being so frustrated because our relationship, for the first time, felt like work. And, in my naïve 20-something year old mind, *relationships shouldn't be this much work* – and this was supported by the fact that it was a relationship which had never required any work up until that very moment. Clearly, this was before I knew that *relationships take work.*

In a moment of rashness, I said the words "I am not going to fight with you."

I believe the words she subconsciously heard were "I'm not going to fight *for* you."

Then, in a very *Ross and Rachel "we were on a break"* way, she accepted a date with another guy the following week. I am certain she felt it was innocent enough at the time, but that innocent dinner turned into a wedding less than a year later.

We let complacency set in and it ended us. The water ended up boiling our frog and we didn't see it coming. Everything was so "comfortably tepid" that we didn't feel the inevitable outcome of our lack of precaution.

Netflix and chill killed us. Don't get caught in the same trap.

(NOTE: I was warned about adding this story into this book, receiving advice about it being too melancholic, but I fought back. I find this story to be quite relatable for most people, this "one that got away." The purpose of sharing is not to look like a fool, nor to dampen the mood, but to express a sincere caution to check the equity in all your relationships. Course correct sooner than later. Be vigilant.)

From the CEO's Desk

Every year, around Christmas, I get a phone call from the CEO of one of our oldest clients. I have little interaction with him throughout the year, but every year he calls me to talk about our staff's performance on his account. He is the only person to do so, but it makes me smile every year.

Prior to the conversation, he always asks for a complete list of everyone who works on his account. Honestly, the list is extensive, but we always provide it to him. Then the conversation begins with him asking me questions about each individual. He has never met any of them, nor ever will, but he wants to feel a human connection to the people.

He continues to ask me questions about how *his* company can do more for *them*. Do they feel valued by his company? Do they enjoy working on his account? Do they have personal connections to his brand? Then comes the question: How can we show them appreciate this year more than last year?

This man has provided *my* staff people with $500 gift cards to department stores. He has sent other gifts too, but he is always trying to find ways to show how much he appreciates them. My relationship with him aside, he wants our people to know how much he values their work.

Needless to say, they love working on his account. His concern for them shows – tangibly. Their concern for him shows in return.

RYZE-ING TO THE OCCASION

Around our place, we function very much like a family. It's our culture, truthfully, and it makes for a very positive work environment. Like all families, however, we get too comfortable. We're fortunate to have a vice president of operations who keeps us in line - but is a big fan of happy hours.

At least monthly, our team is invited to some happy hour event. It isn't about the drinks and appetizers. We schedule random things, all with voluntary attendance, and just provide a space for our people from different departments (and different floors of the building) to interact. To laugh. To crack jokes at each other and build camaraderie. We show our appreciation in random ways, but the building of relationship is the greatest way to show our investment in the people.

It isn't "team building" and "company party" stuff. It is casual and simply provides time to grow relationships. Not only do we find that it makes people enjoy work a bit more, but it also tears down the departmental walls between people who would never have otherwise asked a question or raised a concern.

Today's Lessons Learned

- In personal and professional relationships, it is necessary to continually nurture the relationship with intention.
- Typically, intentional care is met with reciprocity. When affection and appreciation is given, in a healthy relationship, it is given in return.
- Getting too comfortable in a relationship is not a badge of honor. In fact, it is usually a sign of something terrible on the horizon.
- Distraction is the greatest enemy of intention. Don't let your priorities become compromised by something new and shiny.

Now, Ask Yourself

- Self, how do you show the most valuable people in your life how much you value them? How can you get better?
- Self, when signs of trouble appear, how intentional are you about stopping them from festering or becoming dangerous?
- Self, do you recall a time when a relationship slowly fizzled into irrelevance? What happened? How would you have handled that differently had you seen the signs?
- Self, what is the best way in which another person has made you feel valued? How can you use that same strategy to do the same for someone else?

On keeping it together.

CHAPTER 17: COMMITMENT ISSUES

Admit it. Some of you flipped to the table of contents and just fast forwarded directly to this chapter. If so, shame on you. Start at the beginning (or maybe flip back to the chapter about "not taking shortcuts").

For those of you who read from left to right, let's talk about that couple who has been dating for seven years. You know who you are. My grandmother would not approve. In fact, she would be muttering under her breath, "Why buy the cow when you can get the milk for free?"

(I just chuckled writing that last line, but it is so true.)

In fact, I'm laughing a little bit extra because I just got off a Zoom call with a would-be client who is literally the character I would use as the super villain, should my life ever be featured in a DC comic book.

But, back to the cow.

Serious question: What keeps a couple from getting married? I hear the excuses all the time about why couples just don't *tie the knot*. And, as a quick Quora search will yield, there are some common themes. Here are my favorite reasons (all quotes, with citations missing to protect the guilty):

- *"I legally have never been married to my husband that I call husband now after 15 years because it's not necessary it's just* a piece of paper." (Sweet, Lord, please see that there are quotes there and I am not responsible for the grammar there.)

- "Marriage entails a legal contract and that basically terrifies a lot of people. To get divorced, you first have to be married! Also, divorcees, in particular, are very cautious about getting re-married because they learned their lesson the first time. Of course, that's not to say that their second marriage won't be successful, but they're still leery."

- "Two reasons I suspect. First, becauiwe they think it's the thing to do, protesting that no piece of paper makes a difference in their love. I believe that they secretly don't want to get tied down in case they want out if they find a better partner."

- "Because it's not guaranteed to work and if it doesn't work out you can both just go separate ways."

My head hurts.

It's all very romantic, I confess. I mean, who doesn't want to commit the rest of their life to someone without committing the rest of their life to someone? I continue to scroll through the responses and the most common reason to *not* get married is a hypothetical question: "What if it ends in divorce?"

Well, Punkin, that's part of the game now, isn't it?

I mean, the reason to not sign a contract is because it may end anyway? I mean, why buy a car that might crash? Why buy a house that may burn down? Heck, why go to a hospital, since you may die anyway!?

Commitment issues run rampant, I would argue, in many different areas other than just would-be marital relationships. Ask any salesperson who has tried for months, or years, to close a deal.

My contention is simple: **Commitment requires work.**

If you've picked up anything in the last sixteen chapters, it should be that relationships, of all kinds, require work. Lots and lots of work. There are no shortcuts. There are no escape routes (or shouldn't be). Is it any surprise that people would rather opt for a world where they have complete freedom to come and go as they please? My gosh. It's a world without accountability. (There, I said it. Accountability.)

That answer sounds far too taboo for public consumption but let me provide my compilation of the top seven reasons people claim to remain unmarried.

1. Living together is just more common nowadays.
2. Statistically, unmarried women live longer.
3. Marriage isn't legally required anymore.
4. I don't believe in it.
5. Families come in all shapes and sizes.
6. Weddings are expensive.
7. **What if we get divorced?**

I mean, I understand the sentiments, but is that really the reason for not plunging into the ultimate ice bath with your soul mate?

While researching for this book, I took the time to ask various unmarried couples their opinions (promising to never disclose their responses to their partners). Overwhelmingly, one partner would report that he/she would prefer to be married, but the other just "wouldn't commit." And it was *immediately* followed by the justification: "I mean, not much would change anyway."

Does it matter? Yes! Yes, it does! I'll scream this from the rooftops. It changes because someone was willing to plant their flag in the earth and declare a commitment to *you*. It should matter. The idea behind that commitment is a public declaration of commitment. It isn't a "share the rent" commitment. It is a public declaration of accountability. Even before the government found a way to regulate marriage, the ceremony and covenant of marriage existed. (If you're interested in being a bit of a history nerd, Google search the "history of marriage." The concept is so foreign to our modern-day beliefs that it may dismantle everything you have ever believed.)

While the phrase "commitment issues" may conjure images of non-committal men trying to remain bachelors forever, there are certainly applications for it elsewhere in life – not the least of which is in the business world.

Entrepreneurs are the cowboys of the business world. They're the play-by-my-own-rules types who love to show up in town and make a scene, maybe kiss a lucky lady, then disappear into the sunset – off to a new adventure. I get this Gene Rodgers image when I think about it. Even a country song comes to mind.

Toby Keith, back in 1993, recorded the song *Should've Been a Cowboy*. And I don't care if you like country music or not, you can read these lyrics and see how they could apply to any entrepreneur.

I bet you've never heard ol' Marshall Dillion say
Miss Kitty have you ever thought of running away
Settling down will you marry me
If I asked you twice and begged you pretty please
She'd have said, "Yes, in a New York minute"
They never tied the knot
His heart wasn't in it
Stole a kiss as he rode away
He never hung his hat up at Kitty's place

I should've been a Cowboy
I should've learned to rope and ride

Wearing my six-shooter riding by pony on a cattle drive
Stealing the young girls' hearts
Just like Gene and Roy
Singing those campfire songs
I should've been a cowboy

I don't know about you, but that sounds like every entrepreneur I've ever met. We value freedom and adventure. Business ownership motivates us to recoil from the status quo and rebuff the working-for-the-man work life. We shun the tired, traditional workspace. We love the chaos of not knowing what tomorrow may bring. We don't stand still for long.   (And if that sounds exhausting to you, imagine being married to one. Miss Kitty lucked out and never knew it.)

The truth is, however, that the most important thing anyone can do for an entrepreneur is to provide them with structure. They want to fly free and flirt with sexy new ideas. They want to be accountable to nobody (which is why "working for themselves" is the number one reported reason people choose self-employment).

As every entrepreneur knows (and hates knowing), discipline doesn't come easily. Write a thousand words a day. Meet with each of your team members each week. Clear your inbox daily. Make ten new sales calls. They're all things an entrepreneur intends to do, but likely will not accomplish.

Business success is, unfortunately for our non-committal heroes, built on the put-a-ring-on-it philosophy. You must commit to daily, weekly and monthly practices. You must commit to getting stuff done, to relentlessly move your goals forward. You'd think that small commitments like these would be common amongst the aspiring business community, but, sadly, they are not.

This rare breed of individuals has immeasurable zeal and unquestionable passion. They commit to authoring books, starting new businesses, hiring a dozen new staff members, or even more, but when asked to make a commitment like "write 500 words per day," it can be paralyzing. The fear of commitment sets in.

So, how can "write a book" sound attainable, but "write 500 words, starting today" sound crippling? So long as the goal is lofty and intangible, it is exciting. It is fun to envision and dream about. We can imagine some heroic, future manifestation of ourselves magically just "making it happen."

As I write those words, the truth of them in my own life is nearly embarrassing. Perhaps you're feeling a bit sheepish reading them. Guilty as charged.

So, then what?

Once the fantasy gives way to the realization that achieving the goal is going to require *hard work*, it loses its appeal.

[Insert marriage metaphor here.]

Success is not a factor of mere inspiration. It is a combination of inspiration and a lot of good old fashioned sweat equity. For those of us who wrestle with this issue of commitment, it behooves us to find accountability partners who can keep us on track toward our success. Depending on the size of the business, even a COO or CFO can help *manage up*.

Make no mistake, entrepreneurs are willing to work – usually to a fault - but the discipline to succeed can give way when the excitement of something bright and shiny comes along. It takes commitment – especially on the days when all your friends are at the beach playing volleyball.

The same *fight to commit* that exists in business is the type of commitment issues that we talk about in relationships too. It boils down to two things:

1. The willingness to acknowledge that hard work is not comfortable, won't be easy, and will require determination.

2. The fear that the things to which we commit could come crashing down anyway.

You'll never change the way an entrepreneur's brain is wired, but those who surround them can provide incremental ways in которых he/she can succeed in harnessing their lust for freedom and achievement. The structure will allow them to experience fulfillment in completion.

Personal Confession

I'm terrible at commitment. I'm the person who waits until the last possible moment to decide anything, somehow convinced that if I make the decision too soon, I will fail to collect all available data to choose wisely. As if, in the eleventh hour, someone will magically appear and share something that will bust open this lie I was believing all along and save me from the worst decision of my life. My failure to make decisions can often cost me, however, as my last-minute plans and spur-of-the-moment epiphanies come at a premium. (I wish a had 10% of the money I've wasted in last-minute flight reservations alone.)

After much time and introspection (and maybe some therapy), I realized that much of my indecision was associated with my fear of failure. If I were to make a wrong decision, it would not only lead me to failure, but to the embarrassment and shame (insert deep-rooted childhood trauma). I avoid decisions to avoid failure.

More therapy revealed a not-so-deeply-hidden need to please people. I wanted to make people happy and make them proud of me (insert more deep-rooted childhood trauma).

My compromise: I hired a coach. I hired a guy who knows me and isn't afraid to bust me on the lip if I don't follow my own plans. While I can't say that he has, to date, told me anything I didn't already know, he has helped to discipline me into doing the little things that make big differences. I share with him all the big picture stuff I want to accomplish; he chews it up and feeds it back to me like a mother bird. Sweet and digestible, I hear my own plans echoed to me in small, attainable pieces. He says, "write 500 words per day." I enjoy telling him I wrote 700.

I've tricked my brain into achieving tasks, but it seems so much sweeter when someone shares my enthusiasm (even if I'm paying him to be excited).

After recognizing this fault of mine, I found a solution. And it works!

From the CEO's Desk

A little bit more about my shortcomings, I'm terrible at following up with details. I get hyper-focused, then devolve into something far different. I'm terrible at daily meetings. I'm terrible at monotony in general. Truth be told, our businesses would be a mess if anyone had to rely on me to repeat the daily grind. They need me to be envisioning, dreaming, and networking (and writing, obviously).

My solution: Hire a COO. She's quick. She's disciplined. And she's capable of making people do what she wants them to do (without rolling her eyes and looking at people like they're useless for not finishing their projects on time). [coughs]

This one hire has freed up so much of my time and bandwidth. Sure, it is hard to let go, but it allows me to *commit* to bigger things. I can discipline myself into accomplishing digestible pieces of important projects simply because I trust that she can keep the ships afloat while I'm distracted.

Now, I can take a day to write. Or play creative director. Or attend networking meetings. Or spend with clients. I can feed my A.D.H.D. because someone is in the background making sure all the trains are running on time.

Ryze-ing to the Occasion

Recently, I attended a networking conference that helped shape some of my perspectives on many things. One of those things came from a speaker on the first day. He said, and I paraphrase, "Your business currently operates in a comfort zone where everyone is "okay being okay." Yet, you are trying to get it to the promised land. What lies between those two places is a chasm of chaos, but only you know the value of crossing over to the other side. To your team, you look crazy. Who would want to go through that mess to dive into the unknown?"

It made sense, honestly. And he continued to talk about how you can try to inspire everyone and team-build your way to the other side, but they'll always go back to the place of comfort as soon as the pep rally is over.

My ears were perked up, hanging on for what he would say next. Then he said it.

"You are not a safe place for your staff."

Safe? I mean, I think I'm the *safest*. But then it set in. The things that I find to be exciting and new and lofty and shiny and audacious ... they find terrifying. They're not trying to take over the world. That's my job. They're trying to pay their bills - and maybe have a little fun doing something they enjoy.

Around my office, I have learned that if I get too connected to people's daily tasks, I will end up deflating their spirits, as we're never doing enough or doing it fast enough.

Enter my COO. I have learned to let her run the daily grind. I can plan and build the business but need to constantly remind myself to let her run the show. And even when she doesn't run it the way I would run it, I need to stay about 10 feet away from the action. It's safer that way.

By the way, that's *really* hard to do.

Today's Lessons Learned

- The failure to commit is less about the person or task to which you are committing and more about the realization that it will require a lot of hard work.
- Entrepreneurs tend to be free spirits by nature. This passion for dreaming needs to be harnessed, realistically, to digestible tasks or the dream will falter.
- Finding people who can hold you accountable to your goals is essential, in business and in your personal life.
- Country music is not all bad. You may learn from it. Plus, those are simply good people.

Now, Ask Yourself

- Self, when you find yourself holding back from commitment, what are the underlying fears? Be honest.
- Self, are you able to commit to lofty, ambiguous goals easily, but fail to finish tedious tasks? What are they?
- Self, rather than trying to play to your weaknesses, how can you recruit the help of others to cover those weaknesses and give you time to focus on your strengths?
- Self, when you are struggling with completing small portions of a project, what is your go-to trick to make yourself perform better?

On making it permanent.

Chapter 18: Settling Down

Here we are, my friend, at the home stretch. We've worked our way through every possible aspect of a developing relationship – and likely every pitfall – to wind up at our hopeful destination of settling down.

There's something comfortable about this idea of settling down. It's as if the stress of the unknowns has been lifted and we're finally able to channel that energy into other things. There's stability in settling down, after all. There's a comfort in that partnership at the end of the day – a certain Robin to my Batman, Ethel to my Lucy kind of "got your back." Knowing who you're coming home to, after all, takes some of the guess work out of the day.

But, as you can imagine, it doesn't come without its own fair share of – what's our favorite word? Work. Just because the ring is on the finger and the deed is in two names doesn't mean that the work has ended. In fact, I'd argue, some of the hardest work has likely just begun.

Throughout the course of this book, we have discussed various struggles – and strategic remedies – which befall relationships. From the initial hunt to the first fight, from the first date to the one-night stand, we've covered it all. Yet, chapter by chapter, themes have emerged which I contend provide the foundation for healthy relationships – relationships of any kind.

Let's break that down a bit and chat through the five most important, overarching tactics required to keep healthy relationships on track. This interactive game of life requires both offensive and defensive strategies, so let's not only nurture the good stuff, but remind ourselves of the ways in which we can avoid the bad.

1. **Identify and make your needs known.** We've talked about the importance of identifying expectations, ad nauseum, but it is equally as important to understand that those expectations are rooted in some genuine need. Think through this: Nobody enters any kind of relationship unless they believe that a need is going to be met (social, emotional, financial, etc.). And the expectation is that the need is going to be met (else, I'm running for the hills). Why would I get involved in any situation if it doesn't meet my need?

   Think about that first date. That first impression. The decision as to whether you chose to even continue talking was based on your belief in the other person's ability to meet some need. The challenge for most people, with respect to sharing their needs, is that they fear becoming vulnerable. After all, sharing my needs exposes my weaknesses.

   Vulnerability is the antithesis of safety. And, like it or not, we all crave the security of not having to fear harm. If you tell your partner about a need, perhaps he/she will judge you (add shame). If you tell your partner about a need, perhaps he/she will intentionally withhold the thing that you desire (add abandonment). If you tell your partner about a need, perhaps he/she will share that information with others (add trust issues). Yet, the alternative to not sharing the need is continuing life with it unmet.

   I sat yesterday with a good friend spending time talking about his business. He is in desperate need of the types of services that my companies offer. We talked through everything, right down to tax returns. I mean, nothing was off limits, because that's just how we are. But, after hours of conversation and such, it became clear to me that we were each holding back and not sharing something about the potential business engagement.

On my own behalf, I will say that I was very awkward about the conversation, which is really unlike me. I value his friendship a great deal, so I was dreadfully obtuse about being direct about signing a deal. I did not want him to think that my friendship was contingent on a business deal – nor that I would use a friendship to "land a client." I needed him to affirm that he understood that I was not manipulating a relationship for financial gain.

He was equally as awkward about his needs, and it was displayed in his resistance to asking questions about pricing. He didn't want to offend me, but he also needed to feel as if he was not being taken advantage of "because he was a friend." He has been through a lot of negative experience with outside agencies, so he is gun shy, understandably.

When we finally started talking – *really talking* – at the end of the day, we both agreed that everything just felt right, and we should absolutely make it work. Fortunately, we're both open about communication, but the withholding likely cost us hours.

Expressing the need at the root can make you vulnerable, for sure, but it is also the only way to allow someone to meet the need. Unless you're dating a psychic, don't put people in the position of guessing your needs.

2. **Communication is essential.** It may sound cliché, of course, but communication is essential to the success of any relationship. It is only through open communication that we can express needs, share fears, provide feedback, and create

intimacy. I would argue that too many relationships fail because the parties involved simply lose touch – which can be particularly dreadful when you're sharing the same bed.

Of interest, over 90% of divorced couples reported that the first sign that their marriage was failing was the noticeable lack of communication. For couples, it was a lack of time together and the devolvement of conversation into shallow, surfacy topics. For business partners, it was the cancelation of scheduled meetings and the avoidance of difficult decision-making conversations.

And, I will argue, this lack of communication typically comes from a place of vulnerability. Nobody wants to be the first person to speak up, as that may lead to *rejection*.

Crazy enough, I'll mention that the most common example of this failure that I tend to see is between parents and their own adult children. If I hear the phrase "they know where to find me" one more time, I just may scream.

Recently, I was talking to a friend of mine who is a CPA. He manages multiple large estates and is often involved in the structure and planning. He was talking about a client of his who is a very wealthy man who is setting up his estate in a very unusual manner. When asked why he was making certain decisions, the man disclosed that he hadn't spoken to his children in many years – although he spoke very highly of them. The obvious question arose, "Why don't you just call them?" His response: "I can't. It's just been too long."

There is a conscious effort which must go into maintaining relationships, and it starts with the first step. The concern, I contend, is that somebody may get rejected. And fear of rejection keeps the vulnerability hiding in the dark, masked deeply behind a wall of pride.

3. **Never underestimate the importance of trust.** I won't bore you and repeat chapter 9, but everything we are discussing here is related to the vulnerability that a person feels when they disclose a mostly-hidden part of themselves. To make oneself vulnerable, it is an obvious necessity that there must be overwhelming trust. If I share my secret with you, you have the power to hurt me.

   It is true in any kind of relationship, I contend.

   In a marriage, we have the potential to expose our worst selves to someone. We are seen at our ugliest and our worst. Everything from our grooming habits to our finances, our secret addictions and guilty pleasures is exposed. We trust that our spouse will keep those things in the privacy of the marriage, but once things begin going south, it is unreal the things people will share to hurt each other.

   In business, deals are signed under the context of "good faith." We assume that the other party both *can* and *will* fulfill their end of the bargain. We pay half down and hope it works. To the contrary, the other party accepts half down and hopes to collect the balance. The transaction is structured that way so that each party is vulnerable at some point.

   We sign non-disclosure agreements before we share trade secrets and formulae. We never hope to enforce them, but we want them in place – just in case. And, while difficult to enforce, the odds of it ever coming to a legal battle are minute (because it is so hard to prove), but we sign those forms anyway.

   I trust my vendors with my business' reputation. I trust my staff with business' operation. I trust my bank with my money. (Well, that one may be a stretch.) The point is that trust is essential. And I have said before, once broken, it is painful to regain – if ever.

4. **Compromise will be necessary.** In our conversation about Friday nights being date nights, we talked a lot about the value of varying opinions. We enter relationships with people similar to ourselves, usually based on mutual interests or experiences, but we only truly thrive when we can maintain relationships with people *dissimilar* to ourselves.

   Handling opposition in positive contexts makes each person challenge their own beliefs. Often, I find that listening to a person of an opposing opinion makes me rethink my own. Sometimes I become further resolved, forced to defend it. Sometimes I realize that my belief was baseless and couldn't withstand the challenge. In those instances, I am forced to change my belief, making me a better person for it.

   In the context of marriage, compromise cannot be underemphasized. Much of our discord comes from a violation of our *preferences* versus an actual offense. Think of the number of sentences that start with the phrase, "I hate it when ..." Personal preferences are important, for sure, but learning the art of compromise is essential.

   In business, we use the word "collaboration." We work on teams for the sake of varied inputs. We put "multiple sets of eyes" on a project to help ferret out any potential problems and design around pitfalls. We understand that collaboration yields a higher output. We can inspire creativity from each other. We can conjure scenarios that others cannot.

   In each example, however, the art of compromise cannot be confused with a sacrifice of core values. Compromise, if you will, addresses the "minors." Core values address the "majors." We are well-served to bend on the minor issues, but never yield on the major issues. And these vary, person by person.

Identify your majors, then work through the minors. For me, I cannot yield on key issues such as faith or politics. I cannot imagine being married to someone who didn't share my fundamental beliefs. Typically, if you're honest, these types of fundamentals spawn many of the minor issues that trip things up.

I have a friend who married a guy who was *clear* that he did not want to have children at any point. She decided to accept it, despite her deep desire to be a mother. She compromised, but not on the right things. To him, this was a major issue. To her also, this was a major issue. They fundamentally disagreed on an especially important thing, him feeling as if he was clear from the onset and her feeling as if he would compromise in time.

Their marriage is a mess.

5. **Choose your battles.** Battles will happen, as we're all painfully aware. They happen in personal relationships, as well as business relationships. Sometimes they happen in ways we never anticipate. Yet, our response can make or break the relationship.

If you're a fan of Shakespeare, you'll enjoy that I take heed in the wisdom of John Falstaff. If you're not a Shakespearian scholar, first, shame. Then, allow me to explain this irony. Falstaff is kind of the love-him and hate-him character in four of Shakespeare's plays: *The Merry Wives of Falstaff, King Henry IV – Part One, King Henry IV – Part Two, and King Henry V.* He is the often dishonesty, cowardly, boastful, narcissistic character who drops truth bombs like it is nobody's business, then leaves the room. He's the guy you love to hate, yet are forced to respect.

King Henry IV – Part One, Act 5, Scene 3: Falstaff is pretending to be dead on the battlefield to avoid a run-in with Prince Hal. After Prince Hal exits the stage, Falstaff rises and addresses the audience. He speaks: *"The better* part of valour, is discretion; in the which better part, I have saved my life."

Often, this phrase is translated: "Discretion is the better part of valor."

If you're following along, this is usually taken to mean that *caution is better than rash courage.* Or, even deeper, *caution is the best kind of courage.*

Choosing your battles is an exercise of temperance. It requires that one learns the art of intent and eventual outcome. In Falstaff's case, he understood that looking like a coward was a temporary loss which served his ultimate purpose of staying alive. In marriage, it is often the discretion to know which arguments are worth having, versus those which serve no real purpose. In business, it is knowing how often you can challenge the client before losing the contract.

From even the mouth of a coward, we can find wisdom.

While certainly not an exhaustive list of "dos and don'ts," the goal of any relationship is survival – in a healthy, productive, symbiotic sense. All relationships fit this profile, so write this down. Create an intention by which you can nurture those whose relationship bring value to your life. It doesn't happen by accident. As we've said multiple times before, it takes work.

Let's work together.

Personal Confession

If there is one thing I have learned in this life, it is the fact that words are non-refundable. They are a one-way ticket on a fast train in whatever unwavering direction they were spewed. I don't believe that anyone forgives, then forgets. They may forgive, for sure, but they can't forget. At best they forgive and adapt.

For this reason, my communication style – particularly in disagreements – tends to reverse engineer any situation before the first word is ever uttered. It is quite intentional, and I acknowledge that it seems a bit detached in the moment, but I seldom use words that I regret. In fact, I could fill volumes with the times I was tempted to take cheap shots and had the restraint to refrain.

How does this work in real life? Allow me the indulgence.

When conflict arises, my first response is to inhibit a reaction. This, in and of itself, takes an incredible amount of discipline, as we all desire the carnal tit-for-tat, eye-for-an-eye reaction.

Immediately, I ask myself one remarkably simple question: *At the end of this disagreement, what do I want this relationship to look like?*

If it is a dating relationship, that question frames as, "Do I intend to remain in this relationship? At what cost?" If it is a business relationship, that question frames as, "Do I intend to keep this client? At what cost?" Even friendships can require these types of decision trees, actually.

If the answers to those questions yield any response which keeps us in relationship, I harness my tongue. If the person is going to be part of my life a year from now, I will refuse to say anything that would make it awkward in the future. I will speak in love and permanence.

The decision to keep someone in my life is a series of micro-decisions. Each interaction is an opportunity to ruin our established trust. Each interaction in an opportunity to offend. Each interaction is also, however, an opportunity to build deeper trust and greater intimacy.

From the CEO's Desk

I feel embarrassed to include it in this manuscript, but I was once dazzled by the lights of celebrity glam. Who isn't, if we're being honest?

Through a series of mutual contacts, I found myself in a position of working on a project (well, several of them, honestly) that involved the world-famous Kardashian family. Glitz. Glam. Spotlights. Me. Finally, where I belonged. (Yes, I entertained a lot of strange fantasies during that period of life. Not the naughty kind, but the aspirational kind.)

At first, it was exactly the stuff that every ad guy dreams of – early success with a celebrity in the story. I mean, who doesn't want to be associated with greatness? I mean, I was only *two* degrees of separation from Kevin Bacon at this point.

Never in my life have I worked so hard to lose so much money.

You must read that sentence slowly. And groan a little in the middle.

Imagine jumping through every hoop imaginable to satisfy the handlers, only to wind up with a pile of promises. Sure, we did some work (excellent work), but it was never enough. Never fast enough. Never creative enough. Just, never enough. And all of it was to be done as "spec work" (in our industry, that means that you do the work first, and if they like it, they pay for it). Hours upon hours of work put into projects that never even got signed. Signed contracts that got violated and broken. Invoices which took months upon months to settle.

It was a nightmare, honestly.

The sparkle in my eye turned out to be Hobby Lobby glitter. And, like only the herpes of the craft world could, it spread *everywhere* throughout my business. Everyone felt the impact of this client's dysfunction. And, if I would have kept my wits about me, I would have declined the business politely at the beginning.

Consciously, at each interaction, I would have to decide if my intention was to continue this relationship. So many battles were chosen slowly and with much calculation. Yet, when the decision was made to stop working with them, it was definitive and fast.

We fell in love and did everything to nurture the relationship, but when it was over, we didn't participate in the closing ceremonies. We moved on.

Ryze-ing to the Occasion

Let me level with you: Dealing with clients is hard. I mean, it can knock the wind out of even the bravest of soldiers. And I don't mean this as a slam to our clients, past or present, because I'm someone's client too, and I know that I'm a royal pain in the *tuchus*.

Our goal here, at Ryze Agency, however, is dealing with all clients' businesses as if they were our own. We consistently ask questions about how we would want the business to be run if it were ours. We stress the importance of empathy with our clients. We know that the life of an entrepreneur is tough, so we do everything in our power to make it less complicated. It is our commitment.

In treating our clients' businesses as if they were our own, we develop relationships. While reverse engineering our outcomes, we know that our job is to ensure that the relationship lasts for a long time. We're not interested in temporary pleasure; we want long-term commitment and guarantee the same.

I guess that's why the vast majority of our business comes from referrals.

Today's Lessons Learned

- Always make your needs and intentions known.
- Communication is key. Never stop communicating, or else you've already made the decision to leave.
- Never underestimate the importance of trust.
- Differentiate between the majors and the minors, then be willing to compromise.
- In the words of Falstaff, remember that "discretion is the better part of valor."

Now, Ask Yourself

- Self, do you stop to think about the consequences of your words before you speak them? In which contexts are you better about it?
- Self, have you ever stopped to identify your core values? Did you write them down and let them guide you through all relationships?
- Self, are you willing to compromise? Do you let your preferences become a point of contest in your relationships? In what ways?
- Self, do you allow yourself to be vulnerable in sharing your needs? Do the people around you know what you need from them? How do you express that?

Conclusion:
Are You Ready for a Happy Ending?

Let's face it, we're all a little cynical about *happily ever afters.* That's the stuff of fairy tales, after all. But is it? Throughout this book, we've tackled some pretty heavy topics, albeit having a few laughs along the way, but all with the intention of addressing some of the hardest topics in any of our lives – from now until judgment day.

We've talked through breakups, embarrassments, and arguments. We've celebrated the times that things go according to plan and even learned the importance of public personas. It's all connected, friends. It all matters.

But, after reading and rereading this book more times than I care to recall, the one truth which stands out to me throughout is this:

Value the relational over the transactional.

Let that be your takeaway from this obtuse adventure. People matter. At home, at work, or even on the highway, people matter. Let your personal brand be wrought with empathy and compassion and tolerance and patience. Let people think of you as the emotionally mature person who brings balance to life's most complicated situations – not chaos. Let your experiences act as a training exercise to save you the grief of reliving the same outcomes twice.

When I first gave a copy of this book to my friend Rusty, the author of the foreword, I had to reread his text response a few times to let it sink in. After a bunch of input, he wrote this sentence:

"This book is on the exact wavelength of your clients, as well as all entrepreneurs. And, not only do I believe that it will resonate with your audience, *I suspect it has actually helped you crystallize some of your own thoughts and beliefs.*"

As an educator, I have frequently said that we teach best what we most need to learn. Maybe that's true. Maybe writing it down helps make it permanent. Mostly, however, I trust that throughout the pages of this book, you, too, will crystallize some thoughts and beliefs. I hope my confessions and mishaps have acted as a vicarious training exercise for us all.

Wishing you and yours all the best on the crazy journey we call "life."

BIBLIOGRAPHY

1. https://www.purewow.com/wellness/reasons-not-to-get-married
2. https://www.petershallard.com/why-commitment-phobia-is-killing-your-business-growth
3. https://www.livescience.com/37777-history-of-marriage.html
4. https://www.psychologytoday.com/us/blog/cognitive-learning-and-skill-deficits/201903/why-people-take-shortcuts
5. https://www.bankrate.com/surveys/financial-vices-december-2019/#:~:text=Playing%20to%20strike%20it%20rich&text=According%20to%20Bankrate's%20study%2C%20households,annual%20income%20on%20lottery%20tickets.
6. https://www.essence.com/news/study-poor-people-spend-more-money-on-lo/
7. https://www.forbes.com/sites/susantardanico/2012/09/27/five-ways-to-make-peace-with-failure/?sh=790f24eb3640
8. https://www.bustle.com/p/11-signs-youre-too-comfortable-in-your-relationship-its-causing-problems-2907361#:~:text=%22When%20you%20become%20too%20comfortable,says%20psychologist%20Piper%20Grant%2C%20Psy.&text=As%20time%20goes%20on%2C%20if,can%20suffer%20as%20a%20result.%22

About the Author

If ever a person existed who can point out everything that is wrong with anything, you've just found him. It's a terrible trait when trying to make friends, but one that always seems to make for successful implementation. Seriously, this guy can find the flaw in any plan – and manages to do it before anything goes wrong. It's really annoying, at first, but if you keep an open mind to the criticism, it's just gold. And having been an entrepreneur and marketer for nearly 30 years, we would be remiss not to listen.

There is no linear way to explain Mark's career path, but between his own experiences and those he has experienced vicariously through past clients, we're convinced there aren't many things he hasn't done. And we're almost afraid to find something he hasn't done, as he is likely to drop everything to go try it. A collector of experiences and knowledge, Mark makes it his life's ambition to try everything at least once. To quote his Facebook page, "Do everything." – Mark Young

At the root of everything, however, Mark is an educator and teacher. Disassembling projects, campaigns, or even financial statements, Mark manages to reverse engineer a solution, then takes the time to teach anyone who will stop and listen. And it is no wonder, given the fact that he holds university degrees in nearly every discipline you can imagine. And if you ask him why, he'll simply reply, "Why not?" Ask about the time he decided to join American MENSA on a dare – and succeeded.

All of that said, Mark's most admirable quality is the genuine concern and ownership he takes of his clients' businesses. If there were a way to give more than 100%, this is the guy would find a way to do it. He works the numbers, then works them again, reducing everything to a metric and finding ways to improve.

"Do the right thing for the client, regardless of the cost. It'll come back to you. I promise." – Mark Young

Entrepreneur.

Educator.

Author.

Philanthropist.

Travel Nut.

_____

www.ingramcontent.com/pod-product-compliance
Lightning Source LLC
Chambersburg PA
CBHW071446220526
45472CB00003B/694